I0486584

Project Management
Head Start

Murillo Cesar Xavier

Xavier, Murillo C., Ed. 2004. *Project Management – Head Start*. Lulu

Copyright© 2004
All rights reserved. Printed in the United States of America.
POD at Lulu.com

ISBN: 1-4116-1726-6

CONTENTS

Acknowledgments

The first time that I thought about writing a book was during graduation. I was fascinated by all the new tools and theories I that I had learned, and as I sat there in my cap and gown, a great urge came over me to put this new knowledge as well as my past work experiences to use for others. When it was my turn to accept my diploma and I heard my name announced, I wondered almost aloud what topic to write about.

I have always been a very curious person and love to learn about as many subjects as possible, and my choice of a degree allowed me to do just that. In the Industrial Engineering course, I was expected to take all kinds of classes besides those in engineering, including marketing, accounting, human resources, and law. To tell the truth, I loved them all!

Later, I worked as an IT consultant, implementing systems and dealing with e-business, which was a whole new world growing right in front of my eyes. Applying the tools and theories that I had been exposed to in school was very rewarding, but I couldn't stay away from the books, reading everything I could find on cutting edge technology and strategies. This love for learning then led me to pursue a certification in Supply Chain Management to reinforce my Industrial Engineering background.

After getting the certification, I realized that I wanted more knowledge, and in fact, that I wanted more than academic and work experiences. I wanted a life experience. That is why I decided to move abroad to start my MBA. Coming to the US to study was an opportunity to learn about a new culture and to be close to the best students in the world. At Michigan State University, I had the privilege of having outstanding teachers to guide me in my journey. In addition, I could count on the support of all my amazing friends and colleagues.

Once more, the course of study I chose contributed to my formation as a business generalist, as someone trained and experienced in a wide range of business practices. There was not one specific subject that was my preference. In fact, one of the most exciting things about studying at MSU was the possibility of taking a dual concentration, which allowed me to specialize in more than one area. I chose finance and marketing in order to complement my supply chain background.

However, when I finally decided to write a book, this breadth of experience meant that I had a hard time deciding on the topic. My education and experience were so broad that I didn't have a preference or an obvious focus.

Finally, I realized what the perfect topic for me to write about would be: Project Management. I've been involved in many projects in several different companies during my professional life. Furthermore, by definition a Project Manager is also a generalist who needs to understand many different subjects and deal with a great variety of issues.

Writing this book was a challenge and a great source of pleasure and inspiration. I have enjoyed every single moment. I could really re-invent myself while researching other authors and interviewing many professionals.

Therefore, it is not fair to thank just a few individuals for helping me with this book. These pages are the result of different experiences and the wisdom of the many different people I had the pleasure of getting to know.

Therefore, I would like to thank not only the professors and staff from the MBA program at Michigan State University but also the great classmates, whom I am proud to call friends. In addition, I have to thank the fantastic professionals at Holcim (US) Inc. who delight me every day with their knowledge and friendship.

Above all, I want to thank my parents, who teach me more than anyone could ever learn in a classroom.

Finally, I want to thank my wife for all her love and support.

Murillo Cesar Xavier
xaviermu@msu.edu

Introduction

> "Managers are people who do things
> right; leaders are people who do the
> right thing."
> (Warren Bennis, 1925)

Have you ever considered how difficult it is to be a Project Manager? The client can be impossible to please, yet your job is to please him. The team assigned to you may not have the skills, productivity, and synergy you need to execute the project, and you may not have the authority to get rid of them. Time, money, and manpower are always constraints to doing the job properly. For these and many other reasons, to be a Project Manager is probably one of the most difficult jobs in any firm.

The bad news is that every professional is becoming a Project Manager. The repetitive tasks in the work environment are slowly being replaced by automatic processes. Computers are taking charge of making payments, controlling cash flow, ordering raw materials, and eliminating from our lives any repetitive task where we can find simple logic.

We can already observe changes in many job descriptions. More and more, companies are looking for leaders and people with teamwork and communication skills to fill their available positions. Instead of repetitive assignments, jobs are becoming a succession of projects.

Throughout my professional life, I have been involved in many projects and worked with several different companies. Based on my personal experience, and discussions with managers, academics, and consultants from various professions, I have been able to identify some common elements of success in project management.

Although every project is a unique case, with its own set of premises, goals, scope, restrictions, and resources, all the specialists agreed on one point: A good Project Manager and a structured project can dramatically increase one's chances for success.

A Project Manager has to coordinate and prioritize several issues. He needs good interpersonal skills to create team unity, solve disputes, motivate everyone, and maintain a good relationship with the stakeholders.

In addition, he needs great communication skills to lead the group, create and maintain schedules, transmit the project vision to the stakeholders, and to give and receive feedback, among other things.

Furthermore, the Project Manager needs to be creative and analytical to allocate resources; balance cost, time, quality, and results; manage scope; and to solve any other problems that may be raised.

Knowing these things, we may understand how difficult and complex the art of project management can be. Many projects fail for simple reasons that could have been avoided with a little preparation. The main reasons for project failure include a lack of commitment on the part of the executives and sponsors of the project; no linkage to business strategy (what makes the project a low priority of the company); poorly formed teams; and bad project scope definition.

This book will introduce the reader to real project management cases, theories, and tools. It will help the reader to understand the main stages of a traditional project.

In this book, we will present three different projects in order to explore the common elements of success. These projects were based on real cases. The names of the companies were intentionally excluded to protect confidentiality agreements. Furthermore, the intention of this book is not to outline the details of each project but to give an overview of the main phases of a project in different contexts.

In the first project, we will go through a Housekeeping Program Implementation conducted in the headquarters of a civil engineering company with 200 employees. Since housekeeping is a quality initiative, the goal of the project wasn't a one-time deal but a continuous effort. The objective was not only to change the company but also the behavior of the employees.

The second project will bring an ERP (Enterprise Resource Planning) implementation. This is a very common experience in the life of many companies. Different from the Housekeeping Project, an ERP implementation demands a very high level of technical knowledge. Besides, this kind of project is usually one of the top goals of any company. Therefore, the pressure for results and deadlines are additional concerns of the Project Manager. Finally, we should remember that many ERP implementations are handled by consulting firms, causing a dual management issue. We have one manager representing the company and another representing the consulting firm.

In the third project, we will analyze a more tangible output. We will follow a Project Manager leading a Research and Development team in the creation of prototypes for a new product line of athletic shoes. We will see that this is not an easy assignment. Besides dealing with a very diverse group involving engineers, visionaries, marketing analysts, and other people inside the company, the Project Manager also has to deal with suppliers and focus on the final customer at every step.

After understanding the nature of these projects, we will analyze the anatomy of a project. We will break it into pieces and understand the main phases, activities, tasks, deliverables, and concerns associated with each part.

Finally, we will introduce some basic and advanced tools and templates that can be used during a project. These tools may be used in many situations. We don't expect to transmit the complete knowledge of any one tool but to offer a brief view of the tools and their applications in order to instigate the interest of the reader. An additional bibliography is indicated for each tool presented.

There are hundreds of tools companies can use to speed up their projects and improve their results. Unfortunately, many companies just don't use them. Maybe it is because they are too eager to execute something and see no value in planning activities, or maybe it is because they get used to doing things a certain way. Therefore, they have a cultural blockage. Their options are limited. The knowledge of basic tools can give a great competitive advantage for any Project Manager, who should work to convince the company and its executives of their benefits.

Remember that the best tools a Project Manager has are his own skills. Someone creative, with sound reasoning, good organization, and communication skills, can react to new situations, learn, and adapt to create his own method of work.

I hope the lessons from this book may help the readers to improve not only their projects at work but also their personal projects for a better life.

PART I
Business Cases

1 - Housekeeping Project

> "I hate housework! You make the beds,
> you do the dishes -- and six months
> later you have to start all over again."
> (Joan Rivers, 1933)

"The employees' morale is low, our administrative cost increases every day, and our processes don't work as they should. Accounts payable can't keep track of the invoices, the engineers never meet their deadlines, and the IT help-desk is taking almost 4 days to reply to a call." With these words, Mr. Ziabtchenko, the CEO, asked Michael, one of his senior managers, to create and conduct a project to improve the overall quality of the company.

It was a mid-size engineering company acting in construction and real estate. It had four branches in different cities supporting the construction and sales of 40 to 50 buildings per year. Most of the administrative activities were handled by the 200 employees in the headquarters. The company had recently gone through a reengineering process and ISO9000 implementation, but even with all these new technologies and improvements, the administrative performance was declining.

The initial step for Michael was to better understand what was going on with the company. First, he decided to analyze the administrative expenses to find the main causes for the cost increase. Next, he followed some of the main administrative processes to find problems associated with delays and errors. Finally, he interviewed some of the employees in order to collect additional information, such as their main difficulties, opinions, and overall impressions of the company.

While verifying the expenses, Michael saw that the administrative cost was around 30% higher than budget due to payment of overtime. Another cause for the difference between actual and budget was the high volume of office supplies purchased, including new furniture, such as archives and cabinets.

During the interviews and the process analyses, Michael realized that the employees were not satisfied with the workplace. The processes were being followed by everyone—but at a very slow pace. Invoices, important messages, requests from clients, and many other documents could be found in piles of paper on the desk of almost every employee. The lack of organization was growing and causing delays in every process.

There wasn't an owner for each process. In every department we could see the same situation. Michael knew that a meeting with the managers to demand changes wouldn't be enough for a sustainable solution. Most of them could make slight improvements to their departments, but soon all the disorganization and chaos would be back again.

Michael thought of several different methods he could use in order to correct all the problems in the organization, but after evaluating the pros and cons of each alternative, he decided to pursue what, in his mind, was the most comprehensive and effective solution. His decision was based on the comments of Mr. Ziabtchenko and other stakeholders who were complaining about temporary and sometimes ineffective solutions.

With this thought in mind, Michael prepared a proposal to implement a Housekeeping Project based on the Japanese 5S philosophy. 5S stands for five Japanese words with the ideals of housekeeping: *Seiri, Seiton, Seisou, Seiketsu,* and *Shitsuke.*

Seiri may be translated to mean "sense of utilization." It suggests the correct classification and selection of equipment and materials for each function or task. It also includes the selection of information and data required for the assignment. This kind of activity frees up valuable space.

Seiton means "sense of order." It means that everything should have its place. It enforces organization in the workplace. It is the old concept of "a place for everything and everything in its place." Each person has to think about what he or she need in order to do their jobs, how many of these items they need, and where they should be located.

Seisou is the "sense of cleaning." The cleaning should be done not only in the physical workplace but also in the virtual environment. The employee should have only the necessary information and data needed to make the required decisions associated to their tasks. The presentations and reports generated should also be easy to assimilate and comprehend.

Seiketsu means "sense of health." The work environment should have good sanitary and hygienic conditions. The scope of this item includes items such as pollution, noise, lights, and temperature.

Shitsuke is the "sense of self-discipline." Quality is a continuous effort and depends on each individual. Therefore, this item emphasizes the need to follow the rules and instructions of the company and to maintain the best practices.

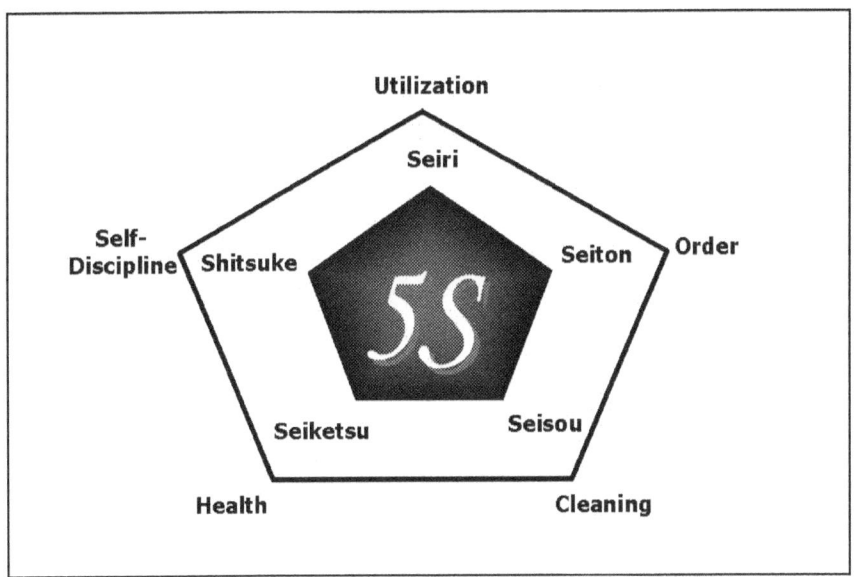

Figure 1: "5S Philosophy"

Once fully implemented, the 5S process reduces waste and non-value activities. Furthermore, efficiency and safety in the workplace increases dramatically. But the main goal of the program is the transformation of the individual. The successful 5S implementation changes the way the employees see the work environment and even their lifestyles.

1.1 – Project Proposal

After evaluating the problems and possible courses of action, Michael worked on a proposal to be presented to the CEO. He knew that most of the employees wouldn't be willing to change their behavior or their workplace. Sometimes, it is a matter of ownership. Some people don't like to have others pointing fingers saying that their desk is a mess and they should clean it. Therefore, Michael had to think of a way to get the real commitment of those 200 employees.

One of the main characteristics of a good Project Manager is good communication skills, and Michael definitely had it. He talked to several co-workers and tried to figure out the one thing that would motivate everyone. After more than a dozen of these informal surveys, Michael realized that there wasn't a single item capable of motivating everyone.

In a very diverse environment, it can be difficult to motivate everyone since each individual has different dreams, aspirations, and needs. Some of the employees were looking for money, power, and promotions; some were looking for a challenge; and others were looking for an opportunity to learn, to be recognized, or simply to be a part of a team.

To solve this problem, Michael proposed a contest with a series of activities in order to tackle each one of the 5S points. Each department would be a team competing in a "Quality Marathon."

Michael knew it would be difficult to control the different activities of 200 employees. Therefore, he selected twenty team leaders. They were the managers and key people from each department. His plan was to manage those twenty leaders and, in turn, help them to manage their teams.

The first activity of the project schedule was a kick-off meeting to introduce the project to all the employees. He would then explain the reasons for that project and show the goals, main steps, and the team structure before addressing any questions they might have.

Next, he would provide the basic training for the team leaders. Michael was expecting to have them provide the same training for their teams. As much as possible, Michael would be present in the training sessions conducted by the leaders with their teams in order to help them and support the initiative.

After the training, the competition would start. Each department would be evaluated in categories such as cleaning, organization, innovation, documentation, safety, and others. Michael created a big list of items that should be addressed during the competition. The list included specific descriptions in order to make evaluations as tangible as possible. For example, computer cables crossing the hallways were a specific item in the safety list.

During the course of the project, there were several checkpoints and reports used to publish the development and achievements of each team. Besides, new communication channels would be implemented in order to ensure that all suggestions, critiques, and questions would be received by Michael. Everyone could and should participate in this process. Michael knew that the main cause for project failure was bad communication. Therefore, he was trying to be available, listening and answering questions as much as possible.

In the proposal Michael prepared, the responsibility of evaluating the work of each team belonged to the leader of a different team. One of the goals of this activity was to improve the interaction among the departments. If people know the responsibilities of those both within and outside of their department, then communication could improve, and consequently, a better process with better responsiveness could be implemented.

Another activity running parallel to the competition among the departments was the contest to select the logo of the 5S Campaign. Everyone could submit as many drawings as they wished to represent the symbol of the campaign. The drawings would be judged by a committee formed by Mr. Ziabtchenko and the board of directors. The winner would receive a prize from the CEO.

At the end of the three months, the results of the competition would be reported to all employees during a small party. The winning team would receive a prize for their achievements. Some other prizes were available in other categories, such as best team leader, best trainer, 5S champion, and so on.

As we can see, Michael was proposing a complex project with many different activities. To present this proposal, he created a two-page executive summary highlighting the reasons for the project, along with a brief schedule and overview of the project with some cost estimates. As an appendix, he inserted the details of the activities with the rationale for them and some data about the current status of the company. After a brief presentation, Mr. Ziabtchenko approved the project, with some minor suggestions for improvements.

1.2 – Project Development

Everyone in the company received the new project in a positive way. In the beginning, they were concerned about the extra work and thought that this was just another initiative of the company to make people believe they were really trying to change. But this time, they could see some benefits in the project plan. Some of them could see the prizes; others could see the possibility of learning something new.

The project wasn't following a traditional top down approach with rigid rules. The managers would have the possibility of creating and changing their areas, with certain flexibility.

Based on the project strategy and benchmarks presented showing the achievements of other companies, most of the team leaders really believed that the project could improve the company and the lives of the employees.

After the project kick-off meeting, Michael scheduled individual meetings with all the team leaders to sell the importance of the project. He tried to map the expectations of the leaders, offer support, ask for suggestions, and assure them that he would be available to support the actions of their departments.

During the course of the project, Michael tried to visit the departments and talk to the employees as often as possible. In one of the visits, he realized that Arnold, one of the team leaders, was not committed to the project. In spite of all the efforts made by Michael, he couldn't achieve the motivation of that manager. He tried to talk to Arnold and understand the reasons for his reluctance in participating. The manager replied that he was too busy with his work and that the 5S Campaign wasn't a priority for him.

Michael thought about electing a new leader for his position, but he believed that this would be a big drawback for the project. Arnold was a natural leader. He was the kind of guy everyone likes to hear and takes as an example. Michael could ask Mr. Ziabtchenko to have the manager work in the 5S Campaign, but that kind of top down approach was one of the things that he was trying to avoid. That kind of attitude might generate a greater dissatisfaction and make people turn against what they were trying to accomplish.

Michael also tried to talk to Arnold, offering support and additional resources to help him during the project, but the manager refused, saying that he couldn't delegate his responsibilities. He was one of those very difficult customers. Therefore, Michael had a big problem: a key person who wasn't willing to have the 5S project as one of his top priorities.

The only way for Michael to revert that situation was to motivate that manager so that he would believe in the importance of the project. They talked for some time about the project and its benefits, but the team leader wasn't willing to change his priorities.

Michael concluded that if he couldn't motivate him at a professional level, he would have to try to reach him on a personal level. He had known that manager for some months, and they had had the chance to talk a little about their personal lives. Michael also inquired about the manager to his subordinates. Michael was trying to map the personality of that leader.

Michael discovered that Arnold was very proud of his accomplishments and that he had great respect for the CEO. He wasn't just a boss for him but also a friend and his fishing buddy. With this information, Michael went to talk to Mr. Ziabtchenko and asked for his help in executing a plan to motivate Arnold.

The next day, Mr. Ziabtchenko was visiting the departments and talking to the managers when he met the problematic team leader. Once there, the CEO saw the piles of paper on the desks, the books on the floor, and all sort of notes fixed to the walls of the cubicles. Looking at that, Mr. Ziabtchenko said he knew that Arnold wouldn't be able to execute all the tasks in the 5S project on time. He made an analogy of Arnold's fishing performance and his poor 5S developments. "Arnold, when you learn the 5S philosophy you will be able to catch the big fishes," said Mr. Ziabtchenko. Finally, Arnold reacted to the challenge of the old friend and bet a bottle of whisky that he would be on time for all the remaining activities and checkpoints. The CEO accepted the bet and said he would be happy to lose it.

One week later, Arnold was the best example of the 5S spirit. His department was clean and organized. Even the way they were answering the phone was more professional and polite. It was an amazing change. In fact, that department wasn't just on time but the first one to finish all the tasks for the rest of the project.

Walking through the departments and talking to the leaders and team members was a very important activity for Michael. Thanks to that, when he became aware of several problems, he could act fast to correct them. Talking to the people also allowed the Project Manager to evaluate at what degree everyone was really assimilating the 5S concepts.

Michael felt rewarded when one of the accountants of the company came to him asking for a copy of the movie used during the training sessions. He said he liked the concept so much that he was going to implement the same project at his home by teaching his children. At that moment, Michael realized his plan was working. He was really changing the way people behaved. He had been able to go beyond the boundaries of the company and reach the person.

The teams were doing a great job implementing all the changes in their areas. To show some commitment from the company side, many new initiatives were started. For example, the hallways and meeting rooms were cleaned more often and redecorated, the bathrooms were refurbished, and the IT department began investing in ergonomic equipment. Even an interdepartmental commission was created to promote integration through social activities.

The contest for the logo of the 5S Campaign brought more than 100 participants to the table. The drawings were collected in such a way that no one would know the name of the author. They would be identified only by numbers until the final judgment. The winner was a lady from the Treasury Department. She knew that Mr. Ziabtchenko had just become a grandfather, so she drew a nice teddy bear hugging a heart that read "5S." The CEO was really enjoying being a grandfather and, in a certain way, his vote influenced the vote of the other directors.

After the awarding ceremony, all the works were placed on the walls of the cafeteria as a way of recognizing the efforts and dedication of those involved.

1.3 – Project Results

At the end of three months, the company was completely different. Once more, Michael analyzed the administrative expenses, the processes, and all the other items that were the initial focus of the change. The numbers were impressive.

Here are some of the benefits measured at the end of the project:

- ✓ 30% reduction in administrative costs

- ✓ 80% less over-time

- ✓ The creation of a central storage for office suppliers in opposition of individual stocks, resulting in a smaller inventory and more available space

- ✓ More than 800 lbs of spoiled equipment and office supplies were thrown away

- ✓ 16 business reports were unpublished to eliminate unnecessary redundancy

- ✓ 33 other reports were sent only to the necessary people, saving hundreds of dollars by avoiding useless copies

- ✓ Creation of a central library

- ✓ More than 1 ton of garbage was thrown away from cabinets and drawers

- ✓ 500 Gbytes became available on the network by deleting files that were no longer necessary

- ✓ Cycle time for payments, customer inquiries, and others decreased by an average of 30%

- ✓ Accounting closing time was reduced from 5 to 3 days

Michael put those numbers together in a brief report with pictures of the office before and after the project. This report was distributed not only to the CEO and directors but also to the team leaders, showing the pay-off of the good job they had done.

Later in the year, the campaign was cited in many intern employees' satisfaction surveys as being the main cause of company pride and one of the most important actions of the year.

After the celebration party with all the employees, Michael started planning the next steps. Based on the results of the 5S Campaign, the CEO asked him to plan the rollout of this initiative to the construction sites and other branches, as well as to work on a maintenance plan to ensure that the 5S Philosophy would be alive in the minds of all employees.

2 – ERP Project

> "Science and technology multiply
> around us. To an increasing extent they
> dictate the languages in which we
> speak and think. Either we use those
> languages, or we remain mute."
> (J. G. Ballard, 1930)

In that South American country, the telephonic companies were the property of the state until the late '90s when a new law opened the market for international investments and allowed some of the companies belonging to the state to be purchased by private parties.

One of the largest telephonic companies decided to sell their cellular business to an international group. The cellular segment was a fast growing business, counting on 8 million clients and solid revenues.

In this deal, the cellular business would still be using all the IT systems of the fixed telephonic company (responsible for land lines) for six months. After that, they would have to be able to operate their own systems, including financial, sales, material management, and others.

Therefore, the company sent a request for a proposal (RFP) to many consulting firms. David was one of the consultants in charge of evaluating the needs of the telephonic company and preparing the proposal.

The RFP presented the situation of the company and asked for quotes for an Enterprise Resource Planning (ERP) installation. ERPs are software tools that integrate several solutions into a single package. Instead of using systems from different vendors to handle accounts payable, project management systems, controlling, investment management, asset accounting, sales, and others, an ERP brings everything together in an integrated database. The benefits of this kind of solution include fewer interfaces, no duplicity of data in the system, and real time data.

Since an ERP is not simple plug-and-play software, it usually requires a large team to configure it to reflect the company's business structure and processes. A team of specialists with experience in this kind of project can dramatically speed up the implementation.

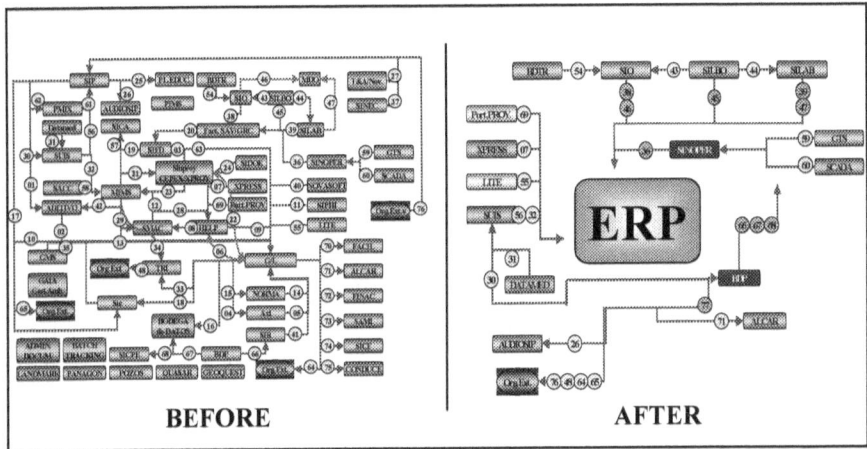

BEFORE   **AFTER**

Figure 2: System Landscape before and after an ERP implementation

In Figure 2, we can see an example of a system landscape before and after an ERP implementation. Each box represents a different system, which the company must maintain and operate. The arrows represent interfaces or manual procedures. It is clear that an ERP drastically reduces the number of interfaces and parallel systems in a company. Besides, each system may require a different treatment for maintenance since they may be written in different languages. Therefore, an ERP also helps to establish a standard treatment to manage the system landscape.

2.1 – Project Proposal

Creating a proposal for an ERP implementation is a very delicate operation. This kind of system affects many areas and any misunderstanding about scope, processes, and other constraints may cause huge distortions in the schedule and cost presented on the proposal. Therefore, most of the consulting companies send consultants with broad experience to evaluate the company and the details of the implementation.

David's first goal was to meet the high management and understand their expectations. He conducted a quick interview with each person responsible for the main areas of the company. Most of them expressed a similar concern about the new system. The company had been working with the same old system for more than twenty years. Consequently, all the managers were concerned about the big changes that were coming. Most of the employees had been with the company for more than fifteen years and might not accept change so easily.

Each of the interviewees also talked a little about the main processes, structures, and systems they were currently using. The CFO, for example, talked about the old asset accounting system. It had a list of more than 80,000 items located in hundreds of different cities. Some of the items were so old that the CFO doubted their existence.

One of the goals of the implementation was to fix all the problems associated with bad data. The new system should have reliable information. Otherwise, according to the CFO, they would only be switching from "an old, problematic system to a new, problematic system."

David spent another couple days talking to the operational managers indicated by the direction of the company. Each one helped him to understand the main processes and constraints under which they operated.

Based on the data collected through the interviews and analyses, David was able to define the needs of the company regarding the system to be implemented. Then, he performed an adherence analysis to match the current processes of the firm with those covered by the main ERPs available in the market. The adherence analysis was based on a tool developed by the consulting firm to help the consultant to evaluate which ERP would better attend to the needs of the company.

Once he identified a suitable ERP, David analyzed the scope of the project. First, he defined the geographical and hierarchical structure to be included in the project (e.g., business areas, regions, and units). Next, he defined which business processes should be covered by the ERP and consequently the modules of the ERP (e.g., finance, controlling, sales, and production planning), which would be implemented.

David also considered the necessary interfaces, data conversions, bolt-ons (packages that are not part of the ERP but should be included in the scope in order to attend to the requirements of the business), and special reports and forms required to maintain the company business. In addition, he drew some conclusions regarding necessary enhancements or adjustments to the standard functionalities of the ERP. Finally, David evaluated the necessary technology infrastructure needed to support the implementation and post-implementation routines (e.g., hardware, software, network, and servers).

Based on time, cost, complexity of the solution, and scope, David suggested a Phased Implementation Strategy. This means that the ERP functionalities would be implemented in two or more distinct moments. In the first phase, only the basic functionalities/modules would be implemented. In subsequent phases, the remaining functionalities of the ERP would be implemented. During the period in between the phases, some temporary interfaces and manual processes would be used to support the necessary operations of the company.

Another criterion used for deciding on a Phased Strategy was the expectation of the CFO. The decision was to load into the ERP only good data to ensure that the project wouldn't be changing the tool only to leave the same old problems. Therefore, the client would be responsible for verifying all of their data before loading it into the new system.

For example, they would have to conduct a physical inventory analysis to ensure the existence and conditions of the 80,000 items treated as fixed assets by the company. This would be an activity parallel to the project. To ensure that it would not impact the project schedule, interfaces would be created between the ERP and the legacy Asset Accounting system. Only after the asset database was cleaned would it be incorporated into the ERP.

In the proposal, David described the necessary number of consultants and staff needed to develop the project. The teams would be divided according to the function they would be implementing. Their sizes were proportional to the complexity of the functions. To manage the project, David was requesting four consultants and their respective partners within the client's organization.

There would be a Project Manager, an Information Technology Manager, a Change Management Manager, and an Integration Manager. The Project Manager would be responsible for coordinating all the activities and strategies of the project—this would make him the one ultimately responsible for the results of the project. The Information Technology Manager would take care of the architecture of the new system, hardware, backups, authorizations, and other technical concerns. The Change Management Manager would be responsible for all the activities designed to smooth the transition between the old way of doing things and the new "ERP way." Finally, the Integration Manager would coordinate the integration activities among the teams and ensure that all of them would be working with the same goals and standards.

David also highlighted the fact that the correct costs and specifications of the necessary IT infrastructure would depend on a battery of tests conducted by the Information Technology Manager. Although the cost of these machines would be the responsibility of the client, David was able to show a cost range of the infrastructure based on other projects.

David's conclusions and notes were taken back to the consulting firm, where he counted on the support of some other specialists to write the final proposal. Besides all the considerations regarding scope, project structure, proposed solutions, implementation strategies, project requirements, and all the financial information, the proposal also described the main qualifications of the consulting firm, their work methodology, tools, and additional information.

Before presenting the final proposal, David scheduled a "conceptualization workshop" with the high executives of the client company. He wanted to confirm his perception of the company, processes, and requirements, and introduce the proposed solution. This was designed to be an interactive meeting where the participants could adjust the proposed solution. After some changes in the original concept, David sent the final proposal.

Some days later, the client replied that their proposal had been accepted. The contract was finally signed and, because of his experience and empathy with the client, David was invited to be the Project Manager.

David's first concern was the team selection. He knew that this activity would have a great impact on the entire project. Since an ERP project usually requires professionals from many areas of the company, some firms get concerned with the fact that these professionals won't be easily accessible to help on the daily activities of their own areas. Therefore, some companies choose professionals that are available, have low decision-making power, and only a basic knowledge of the company.

During the initial preparation of the project, David had several meetings with the executives of the company and tried to convince them of the importance of a good and well-prepared team. The ERP would be used as the main tool of the company. Therefore, the correct definition of processes and business scenarios were essential to the success of the project.

David suggested that the company allocate their best employees to the project in order to ensure fast decisions and an accurate definition of the processes. The client agreed with his points and selected the best managers and analysts they had to help in the implementation.

2.2 – Project Development

In the first team meeting, David presented the goals of the project. Most of the consultants had already worked together in other projects, but it was a good moment to get to know the new faces. That kind of integration before the project was a very common activity used to get everyone acquainted and ready to talk to the clients.

The kick-off event was conducted at the conference facilities of a hotel away from the company. The CEO, CFO, and other important guests spoke to the project team (consultants and client staff). In addition, there were several team building exercises and, of course, the presentation of the project itself, highlighting goals and expectations.

While the team was learning about the project and improving their bond, the company was arranging the physical location of the project as well as desktops, phones, and office supplies.

Two of the top priorities of the first week were to finalize the Risk Assessment Map and the Project Charter. In order to do that, each team analyzed their high level work plan and transformed it into a more detailed work schedule.

With the new work plan, it was easier to analyze the needs of each team, the functionalities being implemented, the interfaces, and so on. Based on that, the management team was able to identify the risks associated with the main activities and estimate the impacts, possible mitigating actions, and contingency plans needed for each of them.

The Project Charter included all the information about scope, teams, risks, project schedules, resources, human resource management plans, implementation strategies, change management strategies, and budget. It was a thick document with the project guidelines, including much of the information described in the contract between the consulting firm and the client.

Another important goal of the first week was the training of the project team. Although most of the consultants already had a good knowledge of the ERP, the staff of the telephonic company had had no exposure to it. Therefore, they needed a crash course to start the project. By understanding the basic concepts of the ERP, they would be able to help the team to configure the system.

In fact, only part of the training of the project team was planned to be delivered at the beginning of the project. There were additional training sessions at some other specific points in time where a necessary knowledge would be required.

All the training was conducted by the ERP supplier. This would ensure that the clients were receiving a complete standard training. If the consulting company were conducting the training, they could try to focus only on specific points relevant to the telephonic company. Although this could be less costly and more efficient, there was the risk of restricting the client staff to a partial view of the system. Consequently, the management team agreed to provide the standard training delivered by the ERP vendor.

During the first week of the project, all the team members were also trained in the documentation templates. During the course of the project, they would have to document several items such as configurations, tests, reports, and the user's guides. Furthermore, the documentation training included the presentation of the database the project team would be using to control any open issues raised by the teams.

After the initial training, all the teams started the configuration of the ERP. Each team had a different working method. Some of them had a person dedicated to documenting the entire configuration. Others had each one documenting only the configuration they were executing.

In some teams, daily meetings were conducted in order to discuss the details of the processes and to define responsibilities for configuring the system with those details. Other teams had weekly meetings, and one of them decided to meet only when one of the team members had an issue relevant for the whole team.

David was following the work of each team, talking to the team leaders and members, and trying to track their progress and help them with any problems. The Project Manager had weekly meetings with all the team leaders, where he and the other managers emphasized things such as scope, schedule, team work, and relationship with the client.

In the second week of the project, David talked individually with each consultant in order to evaluate their expectations regarding career and professional development. He was trying to see how comfortable each consultant was with their roles in that project and how it would contribute to their careers. Based on that, David made small changes in the roles of some of the consultants and used those conversations as a basis to define the evaluation criteria of each one. During the project, he maintained periodic contact with each consultant in order to give feedback and to verify that their individual expectations were being reached.

Another critical activity was the installation of the IT environment. The initial specification of the server needed to run the ERP was based on the number of users, physical assets listed in accounting, different materials the company handled, vendors, customers, organizational structures, and other relevant data to assess the processing capacity of the machine.

The IT managers defined a system landscape with three environments. Each environment would be composed of a full collection of the data necessary to operate the system. It was just like having three different systems.

The first environment would be the "Configuration Environment." Here, the project team would be able to create and test their configurations. If the configurations were approved by the client, the IT staff would copy those parameters to the second environment called "Quality." This environment would have only the approved configuration and would be used for training and final tests. If the final tests were approved by the client, the configuration would be copied to the third environment, "Production." This would be the place where the company would actually be working.

Figure 3: IT System Configuration Strategy for an ERP implementation

Although both Project Managers were responsible for the budget of the project, some unpredicted expenses had to be negotiated between both parts. According to the nature of the expense, the Project Managers could try to request a budget increase from the telephonic company or from the consulting firm.

Some unpredicted expenses involved the training and charges for two new consultants. One of them was called to the project due to a last minute request from the sales division. They wanted a non-standard report to be developed in the ERP. Since that request was not pointed out in the initial phase of the project, the telephonic company agreed to pay for the rates and any necessary training of the new resource. On the other hand, the other resource was called to replace another consultant who quit his job at the consulting firm. Therefore, David analyzed his budget and agreed to pay for the training of the new replacement.

The project management team had weekly meetings to discuss the financials of the project. During these meetings, the financial forecast was evaluated against the project schedule.

Based on the performance of the teams, the Project Managers tried to adjust the forecast and estimate the results of the project. These analyses were presented monthly to the directors of the company who were part of the Steering Committee, a group formed by the high executives of the company to evaluate the progress of the project and help with any decisions, which could cause relevant changes in goals, scope, strategy, or structure of the project.

Kyle, the Integration Manager, spent a great part of the project in meetings with the teams to understand the points of integration between the modules in the design of the ERP. He tried to make sure everyone was receiving the right information in the right format. Besides, he was making sure that no process or detail had been left out.

Most of the time, the Integration Manager was the first one to identify bottlenecks. Every so often, one team had a hard time defining a specific format or configuration of a process in the ERP. That would usually impact the work of other teams.

One good example of a bottleneck was the definition of the Chart of Accounts. Since the company would handle only the cellular services, many of the accounts of the old telephonic company wouldn't be necessary anymore. Therefore, the accountants were creating a new chart of accounts. The problem was that all the other teams needed the accounts to configure sales, inventory movements, purchases, and other business processes.

Kyle acted fast, asking the teams about the main accounts they needed set up in order to start their work. Those accounts were the first put into the system by the Finance team. After that, the Integration Manager conducted several other meetings between Finance and the other teams to define the remaining accounts that would be part of the Chart of Accounts.

Marina, the Change Management Manager from the consulting firm, worked with her pair in the telephonic company in order to identify the main decision makers and influencing people in the organization. They conducted research and interviewed those people to define their willingness to accept the new system. They also prepared presentations, conducted workshops, distributed newsletters, and developed a website with all the information and benefits of the project. In addition, they helped the Project Manager with the progress reports to the Steering Committee and to organize all the training initiatives.

Specialists representing the ERP vendor were called to perform quality checks on the project. They evaluated the structure and experience of the functional teams and management team, the functionalities being implemented, the analyses of the current situation, the future design of the organization, the interfaces, all the identified gaps between the processes and the system, and many other points. It was a very thorough analysis conducted by a third party to ensure that the project was on track. Furthermore, as a result of these quality checks, the evaluators made some recommendations regarding how to treat specific issues and which activities would need more attention.

After all the configurations were ready, the Integration Manager organized the final battery of system tests. Every team started the tests by evaluating the small functionalities and scenarios within their areas. After that, they would advance to the Integrated Test.

The Integration Manager prepared complex business scenarios from one extreme of the system to the other. The teams would present these scenarios in workshops to the Steering Committee and other key people of the organization. For instance, a scenario could start with the purchase of raw material; to the consumption of that material by a production order; to the settlement of the order; to finished products inventory; to the activation of one product from that inventory as an asset in the Asset Accounting; to the depreciation and sale of the asset; and finally to the collection of the money in Accounts Receivable.

The integrated tests required a coordinated action between the different teams (e.g., Finance, Material Management, Production, and Sales). After each small step, some reports were extracted from the ERP and presented to the group to show how the information was flowing through the system.

At the end, the tests were a success. Only a few minor points needed to be fixed. The Integration Manager prepared a document with the processes analyzed and the results obtained. This document was used by the Project Manager and the Change Management Manager as part of their communications to the Steering Committee and to the rest of the company.

Finally, after all the tests, Marina, the Change Management Manager, started implementing the end user training program. They would be trained by the project team with the material developed by them during the course of the project. The training involved expositive lectures about the theories behind the ERP and some practical exercises going through the business scenarios.

In addition, Marina worked together with the IT Manager and the functional team leaders to evaluate each employee who would be a user of the system in order to define the necessary authorizations they would need. These authorizations were also tested during the end user training.

At last, the Project Manager called a general meeting with all the team members, the Steering Committee, and the managers of the telephonic company to announce the transition strategy. Although the transition was a process that had been taking place since the first contact with the client, David was talking about the moment when the company would turn off the old system and start working with the ERP at full power. This event, also known as the "Go-Live," was a very important milestone. He explained what the first couple of days with the new system would be like and how to access the support team who would be monitoring the activities during that period. The meeting was followed by a cocktail to celebrate the achievements and to motivate everyone to the upcoming challenge.

2.3 – Project Results

The Go-Live showed very good results. The system worked properly, and the support team made just a few interventions in the regular operation of the employees. Most of the time, they were helping the end users to remember what they had seen during training. Requests for additional authorizations in the system were also a common problem.

The first day of operations with the new system was a little bit slower than a regular day of work. The users were getting used to operating the ERP. Therefore, they were taking longer to identify some commands and the necessary steps for certain operations. The end-user operation manual proved to be very useful for them.

Each team leader and manager monitored the activities of their respective areas. The IT Manager, for example, was verifying the performance of the system and trying to compensate delays in processes and reports by changing some technical settings in the system.

The Project Manager spent most of his time talking to the team leaders to get their impressions of the main problems each team was experiencing and some other factors, such as users' acceptance of the new system, the performance of each group, and so on.

The consulting team worked close to the end users for ten days after Go-Live. After that, the company started their regular operation with the new ERP, and the consultants were no longer formally available to answer questions about their daily activities. Any new issue would be treated by the Help Desk.

The ERP Help Desk was formed by the users who were part of the implementation team working close to the consultants. Although they were back in their original areas with their original assignments (e.g., Finance, Sales, etc), they now had a dual responsibility. Besides their regular attributions, they were also part of an ERP development team responsible for answering the questions of other users and advising the board of directors on necessary improvements to the ERP. For any questions beyond the knowledge of the Help Desk team, they would contact the consulting firm.

Although the consultants remained in the company for only ten days after Go-Live, most of them returned for specific activities such as the first accounting closing. During this event, they identified one problem with the depreciation interface to the legacy system. It was not automatically posting the depreciation entries as it should. Even after several tests of this interface, it failed during the real operation. The solution found was to make manual entries directly into the ERP accounting system. Meanwhile, the IT team would be fixing the problems with the interface.

Based on the Go-Live results, surveys conducted by the change management team, and inputs from the team leaders, David prepared an implementation review document presenting the results of the project and suggestions for future developments, such as upgrades, new functionalities, and new reports.

All the suggestions and results were presented to the sponsors of the project in a final project meeting. The sponsors were glad to see that all the goals initially set had been achieved.

The end result for the company was a reliable and flexible system. The ERP would allow for the expansion of their business and would support their plans with real-time reports. The transformation of the organization also included the adoption of the best practices available in the market. The transfer of knowledge from the consulting team to the telephonic company was successfully concluded.

After the results of the project were presented and discussed with the sponsors, the Project Manager finalized the evaluation of the implementation team. The evaluations took into consideration the responsibilities of each individual and the complexity of their assignments. Based on that, their performances were judged considering their contributions and results achieved, as initially set in the beginning of the project.

During the performance evaluation, the quality of the technical work of the consultants was also considered, as well as the quality of their analyses (e.g., design specifications, problem solving, and creativity). Factors such as client satisfaction, timeliness, communication, responsiveness, team work, resources management, and others were used to complement the evaluations and help each individual to analyze their achievements. The development of the consultant was evaluated in each criterion based on real examples. For instance, to prove timeliness, a consultant would have to show that he had met all the deadlines proposed in the project schedule.

The final result of the evaluation was a consensus obtained during a discussion of each point between the consultant and the Project Manager.

The last step of the project was the celebration party. The management team organized a project conclusion cocktail to highlight the main results and to thank the project team for their efforts.

In the cocktail, the CEO of the telephonic company also delivered a nice speech emphasizing the importance of the ERP initiative for the organization and making clear that the project was only the first step of the journey. Each day would be a new challenge to learn and improve the new systems and processes of the company. The CEO hoped that all future projects would have the success of the one that had just ended.

3 – New Product Development Project

> "Genius is one percent inspiration,
> ninety-nine percent perspiration."
> (Thomas A. Edison, 1932)

Jennifer was a recent addition to the company. She had come from a consulting firm where she had worked for more than ten years with marketing strategy and product development. The company represented a new challenge in her career. It was a traditional shoe manufacturer, focusing on sandals, boots, social, and athletic shoes. The company had been in business for 50 years. They had developed a solid presence in the Latin American market, covering nine countries and generating yearly revenues of $500 million.

Initial analyses from the marketing department revealed a huge increase in the athletic shoes segment over the next five years. Based on that great opportunity, Mr. Thompson, the CEO of the company, asked Jennifer to support Mr. Lee, the Vice-President of Marketing, on the creation of a new strategy to compete against the Chinese sneakers that were invading the Latin America market.

Mr. Lee had been in that position for eight years. He knew the company very well, as well as the products and the market. However, he felt that it was a time of transformation. Jennifer could bring a fresh view of the market, with new tools and ideas to capture the preferences of the customers. Therefore, Mr. Lee asked Jennifer to evaluate the situation and to come up with a new strategy to face the aggressive competition.

3.1 – Project Proposal

The first step for Jennifer was to assess the current situation of the company. There were 50 models of athletic shoes being produced by the company. The designs and colors used were the same as the first pairs sold sixteen years before. The advertising campaign appealed to quality and tradition.

Jennifer followed the product from the raw materials vendors to the final customer, going through each step of the supply chain and identifying the main players who could make a difference in a market strategy.

Besides conducting quick, informal interviews with the main players of the supply chain, she talked to those responsible in manufacturing, finance, and logistics trying to reconcile their point of view about the future of the shoe industry with their opinion on the appropriate positioning the company should have. Some of them were against investing in a new product line. They didn't believe that the threat of imports was something permanent. According to them, the international freight cost was fluctuating too much, with an upward trend, and in a few months, they felt that it would create a natural barrier.

After talking to the key people of the organization, Jennifer tried to address all the concerns raised during the interviews. She studied the sales reports of the current products and analyzed market numbers and trends, such as freight cost, fuel, GDP of their target markets, and positioning of the main competitors. Basically, she applied the 5 Forces framework to analyze the dynamics of the market, considering competitors, new entrants, buyers, suppliers, and substitute products.

Based on the results of those analyses, Jennifer defined a few different possible courses of action. She summarized each alternative using a SWOT framework. In other words, she highlighted the Strengths, Weaknesses, Opportunities, and Threats of each possible course of action.

Applying the criteria she'd identified during interviews with the key executives of the company, Jennifer proposed the reformulation of 20 of the 50 athletic shoes produced by the company. The new products would rise as a new brand targeting a slightly different market.

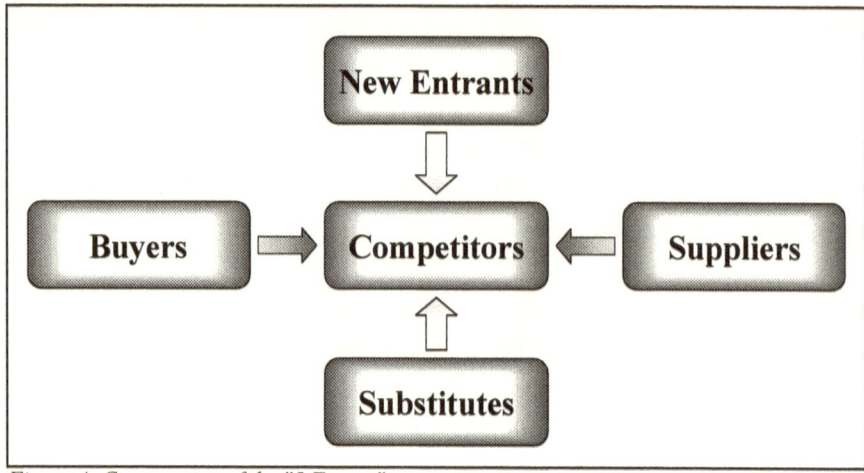

Figure 4: Components of the "5 Forces"

In her proposal, she described the rationale for her suggestion and the reasons why the company should not ignore the threat of the imports. All her conclusions were strongly supported by statistical analyses showing the trends on freight costs, currency rates, import fees, labor costs in other countries, and many other factors.

Although Jennifer's report was showing a very good opportunity for the company, the project also presented some risks, such as changes in customer preferences and the relationship with suppliers and retailers.

Jennifer believed that a cross functional team formed of engineers, designers, and analysts from marketing and finance could develop the new products and a sustainable marketing strategy to launch them. They would also need the support of their main suppliers and retailers in order to achieve their goals.

The proposal included the enhancement of the laboratory of quality control in one of the plants, where the project would be based. Furthermore, Jennifer was suggesting the use of an e-collaboration tool, which would allow for faster contact and the capability of working close to their partners, sharing technical specifications, showing the results of tests, and other relevant information.

A work plan with a high level schedule was also included in the proposal. Besides the activities the team would perform, the schedule also showed many "go/no-go" meetings where the board of directors would decide if the company would still pursue the reformulation of the products. The decision would be based on the new information, which the team would bring from their research studies.

Another important disclaimer on her proposal was the organizational impact that the project would generate in the company. The sponsors of the project had to be aware that the new products and commercialization strategy could change processes, systems, and responsibilities in every area of the company. Therefore, Jennifer suggested that the leaders of areas other than marketing, manufacturing, and finance would have to be involved in the validation meetings as part of a changing management strategy.

Mr. Lee analyzed the proposal and was impressed with the potential of the new product line. He was surprised by the trends of the market and by the fact that the company's market share would quickly fall within the next eighteen months if no action was taken. He reviewed Jennifer's assumptions and analyses and submitted the proposal for approval by the CEO. Mr. Thompson agreed with Jennifer's conclusions and authorized the project.

3.2 – Project Development

Time was a critical factor in the project. Jennifer had a difficult task ahead. She immediately put together her team and let Mr. Lee introduce the project to everyone. The VP of Marketing gave a little background on the origin of the project and talked about the goals and deliverables. In addition, he showed some of the graphs and conclusions of Jennifer's preliminary study to emphasize the importance of the project for the company.

The team was formed of two industrial designers, two marketing analysts, one financial analyst, one industrial engineer, and four interns. All of them were allocated full time to the project. Each one had a well-defined role within the team.

The marketing analysts would work together conducting several studies in the field to capture the preferences of the final customer. They would be working with a specialized marketing agency to help with surveys, tests, and other activities. Their findings would allow the industrial designers to create the designs for the new products. Furthermore, they would be responsible for the development of the advertising campaign for the new product line. One of the four interns would help them with those tasks.

The industrial engineer would represent manufacturing and procurement. He would take the specifications of the designers, analyze the feasibility of the product, and determine the necessary additional equipment and labor the company would need. Furthermore, he would be the liaison between the company and the suppliers. This person would suggest changes in the material used in the sneakers, and, when necessary, involve the suppliers in tests, development of prototypes, and changes in the formulas of the raw materials. Additionally, the engineer would collect all the necessary information from logistics to help the team to understand transportation and stocking. For all this analysis and data gathering, he would count on the three remaining interns. Each one would focus on a specific part of the supply chain: procurement, operations, and distribution.

The financial analyst would work closely with the industrial engineer and marketing analysts in order to get the information needed to estimate the return of the new product line. Consequently, he would analyze all the costs associated with raw material, labor rate, investments on new equipment, inventories, sales, advertising, and others.

The first step after the kick-off meeting was to train the team in the new e-collaboration tool. It was a web-based application where each user could assume a different role in the project. The designers would be able to upload the drawings and specifications of materials and dimensions.

Selected suppliers could be authorized to access those specifications and suggest improvements or answer any questions.

In addition, the system could also generate purchase orders and conduct an on-line reverse auction to look for suppliers with better prices and quality.

The e-collaboration system could also store other documents related to the project, such as schedules, reports, and analyses. It also had chat rooms and other tools for virtual meetings. In addition, the marketing agencies could use the e-collaboration system to upload their reports and verify any changes in the requirements of their client.

In conclusion, the e-collaboration system was there to help with the integration of different areas, project documentation storage, simulations, cost control, and other activities to speed-up and increase the overall quality of the project. However, even with that high-tech system, Jennifer would still have periodic meetings face-to-face with everyone. She knew that human contact was a key element for many fast-paced projects.

Besides the technical training with the new tool, Jennifer decided to conduct a small integration exercise. She bought dozens of pairs of athletic shoes from both national and international competitors. Next, she asked the team to discuss what they liked in each product and what they didn't. After that, she asked them to think about who would wear those shoes. Her goal was to introduce the team to the competition, to make them think about the athletic shoes market, and to encourage them to speak about their perceptions.

That exercise made everyone aware of the challenges they would be facing. They would have to capture and understand the different tastes of the market and develop a product to reflect those characteristics.

Following the work plan, Tony, one of the market analysts, started his research on the preferences of the customer. The analyses done by Jennifer during the proposal phase showed that their target market was formed of customers between the ages of twelve and forty-five; those who jogged, played soccer, tennis, basketball, or volleyball; and those who frequented fitness centers. As per Jennifer's research, this market would grow 7% a year for the next five years.

Tony's initial goal was to get more information about these customers. Therefore, he ordered research completed through a marketing agency in order to find out the demographics, psychographics, media, and product usage of potential customers.

While the demographics would give him a clue on how to find the target customers, the psychographics would give him valuable information about how to approach them. The psychographics would bring some information about the reactions, desires, and other psychological factors that could influence a purchase decision.

The media usage would bring different ways to reach the customers. In other words, it would tell Tony what kind of media would best connect to the person who would buy their product. The results would describe the interaction of the customer with broadcast and cable TV, radio, magazines, newspapers, outdoor advertising, yellow page listings, and many others. Finally, the product usage would indicate to him which other items the potential customers would buy. This would help Tony to create promotions and to identify possible partners.

With that information on hand, Tony saw that he could split his target market into two main segments: students and workers. The students could be divided in two sub segments: high school and college/graduate. The workers segment could be differentiated into three other sub-segments: entry level, middle manager, and senior managers.

Each sub-segment had distinct traits and could lead to different products and promotional strategies. The middle manager sub-segment for example, was formed of professionals between the ages of thirty and thirty-seven, while the senior managers sub-segment was comprised of executives between the ages of thirty-eight and forty-five. Most of the middle managers had two years in college as their highest education, though a great part of the senior managers had graduate courses on their resumes.

The middle managers sub-segment was 267 times more likely than an average person to have never been married, while the senior managers were likely to be currently married. The females tended to represent a smaller percentage in the older sub-segment. On the other hand, the senior manager males often worked more than fifty-one hours a week. In other words, compared to the entire population, these men looked like workaholics.

The senior managers had a household income level between $200,000 and $300,000. The most common household had five members. Finally, most of the customers in that segment lived in warm regions close to the coast. Specific demographic details like these helped Tony with generalizations to later create targeted actions.

We may also exemplify some of the psychographics by saying that in the senior manager's sub-segment, the buyers were influenced by the opposite sex on the decision of purchasing clothes. Therefore, even if the target audience was a male professional, the advertising campaign should consider reaching females too, since they were key in the decision making process.

According to the research, the males in the senior manager's sub-segment were generally risk takers and hated housework. Women in the same sub-segment were happy with their standard of living, enjoyed shopping for clothes, would like to help in environmental organizations, and really liked to cook. Illustrating the behavioral extreme, men didn't want to help environmental organizations and didn't like to cook.

To reinforce the contradictory psychographic attitude conclusion, men tended to be brave and daring, enjoying radical sports, while women would be efficient, organized, refined, and sophisticated. Having a handle on these different characteristics was important to Tony in order to alter advertisements to specific gender related attitudes.

The media usage profile was showing that the senior manager's sub-segment was adequately reached by the mass media. Ninety percent of the group could be reached through seven magazines and fifteen cable TV stations. The research also identified the preferred TV programs.

In conclusion, analysis provided a detailed profile of the customers and helped the team to define the advertising campaign and part of the product line specifications. To get additional details regarding customer preferences, the marketing analysts also conducted other analyses, such as Focus Group and Quality Function Deployment (QFD).

The Focus Group technique is a structured discussion conducted by a moderator. It can be used for reaching many different objectives, but Tony's main goal was to identify specific hidden information requirements, revealing hidden needs, wants, attitudes, feelings, behaviors, perceptions, and generating new ideas about athletic shoes. One important conclusion from that analysis included the color preferences of each sub-segment. Teenagers preferred light and bright colors, while the others had a preference for basic colors (black, white, and gray) since they would wear the sneakers to casual events.

The QFD is a tool used to translate the attributes and desires of the customers into technical specifications. For instance, the results of the QFD analyses indicated that the customers had a preference for shoes which were soft, light, and easy to wash. In addition, the shoes shouldn't have a very high platform. The QFD described the exactly dimensions in terms of weight and height.

Based on all the findings, the designers start working in different shoes for the different sub-segments. The marketing analysts also used the 4Ps framework to define the best marketing plan (4Ps stands for Price, Promotion, Place, and Product).

Since each target market had a different income level, the price strategy would take this into consideration. Therefore, each sub-segment would have a product line with a price range designed to attract them.

The promotion would take into consideration all the psychographics collected. Depending on the segment, the advertising campaigns could appeal to specific shoes for specific sports, or they could try to sell the idea of "single purpose shoes." Furthermore, the campaigns would be directed not only to the final customer but also to the key people who could influence the customer in his purchase decision.

For the sub-segment containing the busy senior managers, a slogan like "Shoes to enjoy your free time" could be used to appeal to their wish of freedom. The different advertisements would be placed in the specific places frequented by each target group. The ads on TV channels and magazines would also be in accordance to the public reached by that media.

In the 4Ps framework, "Place" is where the customer can find the product, and the goal is to generate ideas to make it as comfortable and convenient as possible for the customer to find and acquire the product. Based on the data collected during research and marketing surveys, the marketing analysts realized that a great part of the users were willing to buy athletic shoes on the Internet. Consequently, they proposed the creation of an e-store on their corporate website or a link to an e-retailer. In addition, the salespeople of some of their main traditional retailers would receive a fifteen-minute training session about the product and would receive a free pair to motivate the sales. With the training, they would be able to do a better job advising their clients on the characteristics of the product.

Besides the product itself, the industrial designers were in charge of creating new packages for the shoes. Since the research showed that many customers would take the sneakers in bags to the gyms, courts, or other places, the designers were proposing a package that could be used as a hand-bag or a travel case for the shoes.

While the marketing analysts were working on the research, surveys, and marketing plans, Jullian, the industrial engineer, was supporting the industrial engineers by contacting the vendors and production managers to study new possible materials to be utilized in the production.

Most of the suppliers presented new polymers and fabrics. The new technologies were very resistant, light, and affordable. Jullian took as many samples as he could to the laboratory and worked with technicians to evaluate the characteristics of each material.

Based on the results of the tests and on the preliminary designs of the new products, Jullian estimated that the company would need some small changes in two production lines in order to work with the new materials. He also estimated the production rates in order to forecast the average monthly production volume.

In addition, Jullian realized that two of the geographic markets described by the marketing analysts as a target market were too far from the plant that would be producing the new shoes. Therefore, the industrial engineer proposed the creation of a new, small distribution center close to these markets. The company would save by shipping a bigger lot of products by rail and then use trucks to distribute the shoes to the local retailers.

Mark, the financial analyst, analyzed this proposal from an economic point of view and concluded that the return on that idea wasn't so attractive. However, he advised them to outsource the distribution center. In other words, the company would contract the services of a third party who would provide warehouse and handling at that location. Consequently, the company wouldn't have to create and maintain a distribution center over there.

Jennifer was very pleased with the work of her team. They were very motivated, using the system to share information, and they worked hard to maintain their tasks according to the project schedule. As much as she could, she was helping everyone with the analyses and checking to make sure that there were no communication problems between different areas. Jennifer maintained weekly meetings with Mr. Lee to show the progress of the project.

The project schedule also predicted four validation meetings. The CEO and other high executives were invited to those meetings to validate the results and to approve the next steps of the project.

In the first meeting, the preliminary results of the marketing surveys and analyses were presented. Jennifer showed the profile of the customers, the most attractive markets, and the financial performance indexes for the new products. Based on that, she presented the product strategy; in other words, the idea of having specific products for specific audiences. It was a long meeting with many discussions about the numbers and assumptions made during the analyses, but, at the end, the committee approved her strategy.

The goal of the second meeting was to validate the new product concepts. Jennifer introduced the designs of the new athletic shoes and linked them to the advertising campaign and target markets. Furthermore, she presented the necessary changes in the production lines, raw materials, suppliers, and productive processes in order to produce the new shoes. A complete financial analysis supported all the suggested changes. Once more, the committee approved all the changes and authorized the development of prototypes.

The second validation meeting was especially important. That was the concept freezing milestone. This meant that after that, no significant change could be made to the product. The designs and materials approved were close to the final version.

After the prototypes were created, the marketing team distributed the shoes to a sample group of customers to determine customer satisfaction and acceptance. These results were presented in the third validation meeting. The executives were impressed with the good results and authorized the field test.

The field test was the introduction of the product into a small community to validate the results of the laboratory tests. Besides, this test tried to estimate the trail rates and repeat purchase rates. In other words, they tried to analyze the percentage of customers who would try the product and how many would be willing to repeat the purchase in the future.

In the fourth meeting, Jennifer presented the results of the field test. The high executives of the company were very satisfied with the numbers and approved the large scale production and commercialization.

At the end of the fifth month of the project, the company had been trained to assimilate the new manufacturing processes, advertising approach, product knowledge, and other topics. Following the initial plan, the salesmen at the main retailers were also trained in similar topics.

3.3 – Project Results

The project team and some of the high executives of the company celebrated the first shipment with a nice dinner in the best restaurant in town. The VP of Marketing also promised a weekend in a resort by the beach for the project members and their families as a bonus for their commitment to the project if the results of the first month of sales were satisfactory.

The team carefully followed the results of the first month, monitoring the sales and helping the retailers with the promotional material. Furthermore, they continued to study the opportunity for growth and penetration in other markets.

Jennifer prepared the individual evaluations of the project members, which helped the executives of the company to define their new assignments and supported the decision of offering everyone a project bonus.

Jennifer conducted one last meeting with the executives of the firm, where she presented a report with the results collected during the first month of sales, suggestions for improvements to the product line, the financial performance of the whole project, and a concise life cycle management plan for the new products.

After the first month, the monitoring of the new product line began to follow the same process as the other shoes. Jennifer was nominated the brand manager responsible for the new athletic shoes. She assembled a new team to handle all the new advertising initiatives, requisitions of the market, and the opportunities and threats to her product line.

Six months later, the new product line was noted by the CEO as the main reason they were able to survive the pressure of the imported Chinese shoes and even improve their market share.

PART II
Concepts of Project Management

4 – Project Preparation

A project starts when the necessity is identified. At this moment, a small team is usually put together to formulate the problem. Sometimes they have to find the causes of the problem to propose a project, such as Michael did in the 5S Project. In some other cases, the general goal of the project is already presented by the client. For instance, in the ERP project, the RFP (Request for Proposal) clearly stated the main objective of the project.

Many authors and consulting companies refer to this part of the project as "Design," "Define," "Visualization," and "Preparation." However, almost every time, we will find the same elements in this initial phase. Here are some of the main activities developed in this phase:

- ✓ Identification of Stakeholders
- ✓ Problem Definition
- ✓ Creation and Selection of Alternatives
- ✓ Risk Assessment
- ✓ Infrastructure Plan
- ✓ Project Organizational Structure
- ✓ Project Charter

Depending on the nature and size of the project, these activities may be shorter or longer and even conducted in a more formal or informal way. However, the preparation phase is probably the most important of the project, since it will serve as a roadmap for all the other activities. It doesn't matter how fast you run if you don't know where you are going.

During the preparation phase, we will have several activities involving topics such as Integration, Quality, Risk Management, Human Resources, Communication, Scope, Cost, and Time Management. These are distinct topics that need the constant attention of the Project Management along the whole project. According to the size of the project, the Project Manager can nominate an individual or team responsible for each of these topics, but he must have in mind that he is the one ultimately responsible for the whole project.

4.1 - Identification of Stakeholders

The first step in a project is to identify your client and all the others who can be impacted by the development of the activities. This activity is not as easy and simple as it seems. Sometimes, we focus on a specific person as a client and forget to think about the other people involved. Then, you may end up with a lot of unsatisfied people going against your project.

A stakeholder is anyone interested in the success of the project. Generally, his work will be directly or indirectly affected by the project. Therefore, it is important to identify these individuals and get their support. It is necessary to align their expectations with the goals of the project. We can have internal stakeholders, such as project members and employees, or external stakeholders, such as the community impacted by the project.

Good communication will be a valuable asset in accomplishing this task. Most of the time, the Project Manager will have to translate the strategic goals of a stakeholder into an operational plan. The stakeholder may have different backgrounds and represent interests from different areas. The Project Manager has to consolidate these expectations and goals in order to formulate a solid project plan supported by everyone.

Since the expectations from each one may change during the course of the project, the relationship with the stakeholders requires a continuous effort. The Project Manager should plan periodic interactions with them to keep them involved with the project.

After identifying the key stakeholders (those with higher influence), the Project Manager should try to identify the nature of their involvement in the project. They may be responsible for some activities, the source of financial resources, the role model of an entire department, or many other things.

The correct understanding of the background and context of the stakeholders will allow the Project Manager to map their key projects, objectives, and issues from a business point of view. The Project Manager may also try to draw some psychographics, such as his general perception of the stakeholder, his openness for change, and his readiness for help. This assessment may be done in an informal way and be part of the personal files of the manager. Some consulting companies have a spreadsheet ready with several factors, which they try to evaluate. At some degree, they are similar to the interview guides human resources uses to evaluate a candidate.

In the third part of the book, we give an example of a simple template of a perception map that can be used and adjusted according to the project.

In our Housekeeping Project, Michael identified not only the CEO but also all the employees of the company as stakeholders. He tried to collect their opinions and combine their expectations in order to develop a project plan that would be accepted by everyone. The project would probably have been a disaster if Michael had used only the expectations of the CEO in order to develop the project strategy. We could also see how important the stakeholder assessment was when Michael had to persuade one of the team leaders to embrace the project. Furthermore, the correct identification of the stakeholders allowed Michael to effectively report the developments and results of the project.

To know the mind of the stakeholder is a great competitive advantage. In the Housekeeping Project, for example, the winner of the logo competition correctly identified the main stakeholder and his preferences. That creates an initial advantage for the contestant who actually won the competition.

Most of the time, the stakeholders have secondary objectives or constraints that are not clearly stated anywhere. In the ERP project, we saw that thanks to the interviews with the stakeholders, David realized that the goal of the project was more than just the implementation of the system. The stakeholders were also looking for a way to fix existing managerial problems and to have access to reliable information. Furthermore, the interviews highlighted the importance of a good change management strategy, since many of the employees wouldn't be willing to easily accept the new system.

Champoux [7] describes two ways a manager can react to resistance. They can treat it as a problem to overcome or as a signal to get more information about the reasons for the resistance. If the manager decides to view it as a problem and use his power to suppress it, he may increase the resistance to the project. Consequently, Project Managers should try to know the stakeholders as much as possible and the reasons behind their actions.

4.2 - Problem definition

Most of the time, the first thing someone will ask you to do is to solve an effect and not a cause. A client may approach the Project Manager asking him to develop a project to improve their revenue, reduce their costs, improve their quality, and many others. These are basically the consequences of a dysfunction in the company. High costs are generally a consequence of deficiencies in processes, strategies, or some other factor associated with the structure of the company. Consequently, before starting the project, we should pinpoint the cause of the problem.

The inputs of the stakeholders are clues to use to better define the problem. When we sell the project back to them, we have to be sure we have addressed their concerns and show how the project (acting on a cause) will impact the problem they raised (the consequence).

Many tools can be used in this phase of the project, such as the Cause and Effect Diagram (also known as Ishikawa or the Fishbone Diagram), Pareto Analysis, Benchmarking, Force Field Analysis, Affinity Diagram, Flowchart Diagram, and interviews. Each of them may be used to analyze specific effects. A brief description of some of these tools is presented in the third part of the book.

For example, if your company is complaining about high administrative costs, you may try to get an expense report and compare the actual expenditures with what was budgeted for each Cost Center and Account. Then, get the absolute variance and use the Pareto Analysis to identify the drivers of the high costs. After that, you just have to go to the Cost Centers and understand if there are special causes for the expenses, such as a special event or a problem with the initial budget allocated to the department. If the cause of the problem has been repeating itself, then we have to find the reason for that and put a project in place to stop it.

The other important point during the identification of the problem is the documentation of the current status. The Project Manager should define the indicators he will use to measure the success of the project and then document their current status. For example, the total amount of expenses of each department and the percentage of variation from budget.

In the Housekeeping Project, we saw Michael running cost reports and talking to different people to find out the causes of the problems with cost and delays in the business processes. After finding the reasons, he documented everything to be sure that he would have a way to measure the improvement at the end of the project.

For some projects, the correct identification of the problem may require some specific tools related to the area the project is addressing. For example, to evaluate the problem with the strategy of the company in the New Product Development Project, Jennifer used tools like 5 Forces Analysis and the SWOT Framework. Therefore, the Project Manager has to study the area of knowledge covered by the project and learn about the possible tools he has available.

4.3 - Creation and selection of alternatives

After identifying your stakeholders and the causes of the problem, it is time to solve them. To accomplish this task, creativity and analytical ability will be the main assets of the Project Manager.

First of all, the Project Manager has to be familiar with the subject. He has to understand the problem and its effects on the organization. Research, analysis, and surveys, may be necessary in order to better understand the problem and to visualize possible solutions. With this information, the Project Manager may use some traditional tools and techniques to propose possible courses of action.

The results of these tasks may generate many different ways to solve the problem. To define the best approach, the Project Manager should establish clear criteria. The interest of the stakeholders will be the driver of the criteria. The solution may try to combine factors such as low time to conclusion, low cost, high quality, low impact on daily activities, and many others.

In fact, we may even end up with many projects to address different problems found along our analysis. The criteria established will allow the Project Manager to prioritize the projects and select the best alternatives.

The criteria may involve some complex analyses such as IRR, Payback, EVA, Real Options Valuation, and Optimization Models, among others. In the third part of the book, we give a brief explanation of some of these tools. It is important for the Project Manager to work with the stakeholders in order to define the criteria and assumptions used in this phase.

The alternative selected can help identify the expected outputs of the project. These expectations may be used as indicators to measure the success of the project. However, it is important to define SMART goals. This means that the goals should be Specific, Measurable, Achievable, Realistic, and should include a Time component.

Once the best alternative has been defined, the Project Manager can create a work plan with all the necessary activities needed in order to conclude the project. This work plan should include an estimate of the time needed to complete each activity and checkpoints where some deliverables can be expected. A Gantt Chart is usually a great tool to use to accomplish this task. The Gantt Chart is a form of representing a project with the activities displayed on the left in an indented structure and a graphical display of the time frames on the right, parallel to a horizontal timeline.

Most of the software used to construct Gantt Charts would also allow the user to define the precedence of each activity. In other words, it allows us to define the order in which specific activities should be completed and how much time is needed in advance.

The Gantt Chart offers a good visibility of the activities and allows for identification of the critical path. The critical path is the sequence of activities that should be prioritized since any delay in these activities would cause the delay of the project.

Some of the software available for project management also includes a resources leveling capability, which tries to optimize the project schedule, reducing the overlap of activities requiring the same resources. Additional details regarding Gantt Charts and the creation of schedules are described in the third part of this book.

In the Housekeeping Project, Michael studied the best way to attack the causes of all known problems at once. He studied the 5S Philosophy and became a specialist before presenting the proposal to the CEO. He also took into consideration the expectations of the stakeholders who were demanding an effective solution. Therefore, after a good analysis, creation, and evaluation of the alternatives, Michael could present the Housekeeping Project following the 5S Philosophy.

In the ERP Project, we saw that after considering all the criteria defined by the sponsors of the project, David, the Project Manager, proposed a "Phased Implementation Strategy" instead of a "Big Bang" approach.

In the Phased Implementation Strategy, only part of the new process is implemented in each phase. Generally, we have interfaces between these new functionalities and the legacy systems. These interfaces should last until the remaining functionalities are installed in subsequent phases of the project, when the legacy systems are shut down. In the Big Bang approach, all the components of the ERP are installed at once.

4.4 - Risk assessment

We may associate every project with the specific risk of not reaching its goals. The risk assessment is an activity to identify the main events that may cause the failure of the project.

Depending on the kind of risk identified, we may use different mitigation strategies. In a project where the quality of the output is the top priority, we may extend the timeline of the project and add more people controlling the quality. In a project where time is an issue, we may try to reduce the scope, add more people, and work with more parallel activities in order to speed up the project.

Actions such as project budget increasing, changing timeline, and using different structures and strategies are very common in managing the project risk. However, a more detailed analysis is usually recommended to justify such actions.

A Risk Assessment Chart is a very simple tool that may help the project management to make a more accurate judgment about the severity of each threat. This chart consists of a list of the main tasks of the project, a brief description of the possible problems we may find to finalize each task, a proposed controlling tool, mitigating action, and a backup plan. An example of a Risk Assessment Chart is presented in the third part of this book.

For example, if in the Housekeeping Project we had defined "training" as one of the critical activities for the success of the project, we would have it in our Risk Assessment Chart with a list of things that could cause the failure of this activity. Some of the possible reasons for failure could include the purchase of the training videos from Japan or the low attendance of the invitees.

The mitigating plan to reduce the risk associated with the training activity could involve the use of domestic training materials to ensure timely delivery. To ensure attendance, a memo from the CEO could make the training a required event. The backup plan could state that the training would be done with material developed in-house and would be conducted during alternative hours, such as during a business lunch.

After the risk assessment, the Project Manager should be able to reach a balance between performance, cost, and time. Have in mind that periodic reviews are necessary since each new event in the project may impact the risk of the activities.

4.5 - Infrastructure plan

Infrastructure means of the various resources necessary in order to ensure the completion of the project. In other words, we are talking about equipment, physical location, and people. Each project has a different need. However, the infrastructure available may have a direct impact on timeliness and the quality of the overall solution.

Many projects require the full-time commitment of the team members. In this kind of situation, the Project Manager may try to have his team relocated to a different office or room. It should be a place where he and his team won't be easily disturbed by the rest of the organization with requests from their previous assignments.

While selecting the team, the Project Manager should consider the available candidates and resources. A cross-functional team may improve the quality of the final solution, since different areas will have a representative in the team who will be able to transmit their needs and constraints. However, because people from different areas may be used to different standards and have different backgrounds, we may see some cultural barriers, which may affect the timeliness of the project.

In the ERP and in the New Product Development project, we saw the concerns of the Project Managers when they were putting the teams together. They wanted the best people with them. Sometimes, they were not even available, but they tried to convince the sponsors about the importance of having the right people to work on the projects. Important projects with great impact on the companies should have good people on the team to increase productivity and to ensure a high quality result.

The Project Manager should be aware of additional people he may need during the course of the project, such as specialists to aid in the development process and to confirm the quality of the developments at specific points.

In this phase, the Project Manager may create a Human Resources Management Plan to define the profile of the team members he needs, the evaluation criteria, retention plan, motivation strategy, and training programs, among other items.

The correct description of the necessary team members will allow for a quicker substitution in case one of them needs to be replaced. The evaluation criteria should be as tangible as possible, reachable, and directly linked to the success of the project and to the development of the employee.

The motivation plan should take into consideration not only the team but also the individuals. The Project Manager should try to map the motivational factors of each member of his team and use these factors as an asset. Furthermore, these factors can be used in the retention plan.

Depending on the length of the project, we may see a high turnover ratio among the team members. This should be avoided because they have a terrible impact on the schedule of the project and the motivation of the team. The retention plan also deals with strategies to maintain the employees after the completion of the project, since they may have acquired new tradable skills, which may have increased their market value as professionals. Therefore, strategies like job rotations, promotions, bonuses, and training may be used in the retention plan.

Another important factor that deserves some attention in this phase is the Project Documentation Strategy. Depending on the size of the project, the Project Manager may want to document everything. Therefore, he may need a database or space on a network. Besides, it might be a good idea to define some templates. They may speed up the documentation process and ensure reliability and quality by defining a standard for all the necessary and relevant information.

After the definition of necessary people, project facilities, and equipment, it will be possible to create an initial budget. The budget should be as detailed as possible so that it will be easier for the Project Manager to control and justify.

In a project, the budget is usually prepared by the Project Manager in a bottom up approach. In this method, he will break the activities into small pieces and calculate the cost of each component as well as the cost of each resource. This is a good approach, but someone using this approach should be concerned with the "bullwhip effect."

The "bullwhip effect" is a supply chain term used to describe how small decisions on the customer's side may cause a big effect on the upstream side of the supply chain. For example, the customers in a specific supply chain may create their forecasts and add 5% of safety stock. The retailer may receive these forecasts and add another 5% of safety stock. The assemblers may receive the forecasts of the retailers and also add 5% of safety stock. Finally, the industry responsible for the production may receive the forecast from the assemblers and also add 5% of safety stock. At the end, we will have 21.5% safety stock in the system.

In a project, we may see a budget created in a bottom up approach using the input of each team member. The budget may start with the team members and make its way up, going through the team leaders and manager assistants until it finally reaches the Project Manager. If in each of these levels a 5% safety margin were added to the budget, we would have a final number inflated by 21.5%. Therefore, safety margins should be used with certain precautions. It is recommended to use them only at the consolidated level.

The budget may also follow a top down approach. It happens when financial resources are among one of the main constraints of the project. In that case, the Project Manager has a fixed amount he has to allocate among the teams and activities to ensure the completion of the project.

To estimate the costs of the resources and activities, the Project Manager may use different techniques. He may base his assumptions on quotes from the suppliers of the equipment and services the project will need. He may also use standard costs to forecast the total expenditure. For example, if he knows that the rate of a financial analyst is $50/hour and the project anticipates the utilization of that analyst for 200 hours, he may include $10,000 in the project budget.

The Project Manager may also try to estimate the cost of the project based on similar projects and the opinions of specialists.

The project may require specific equipment, which may need to be quoted and ordered in advance. Depending on the quantity of planned equipment, it might be a good idea to use some advanced software for projects, which will give the Project Manager a better way to coordinate all the necessary actions for the acquisitions. Some of the programs combine the project schedule with MRP (Material Requirements Planning) functionalities. It means that the Project Manager may plan the necessity of the equipment ahead of time and, based on the information entered, the software will trigger actions such as purchase requests. Based on that, we may update our project implementation schedule with the cost and dates for the purchase of the necessary equipment.

In the New Product Development Project, we saw the team utilizing a web-based system in order to coordinate their actions and to speed up the communications process. Jennifer, the Project Manager, foresaw the necessity of a tool to maintain better control of documents, communications, activities, issues, and other points of the project. She updated the project schedule with an implementation activity and training of the project team in the new system. The software helped her with many managerial activities and improved the overall quality of the project.

In conclusion, the outputs of this phase are the Human Resources Management Plan, the Documentation Strategy, the Enhanced Project Schedule with the resources requirements, and the detailed Budget.

4.6 – Project Organizational Structure

There are many different structures that can be used while creating the project organizational structure. The organizational structure of a project is similar to a company's structure. We may observe matrix, functional, product-team, and other mixed structures.

The structure is usually defined according to the requirements of the project. A flexible structure is recommended in an environment with quick changes where the decisions can be made in a decentralized way. More flexible structures are also suggested in environments where we have a team of highly skilled participants. Other factors that may affect the organizational structure decision are the knowledge of the team members, the necessary equipment to accomplish each task, the desired level of integration, the implementation strategy, and the responsiveness of the teams, to name a few.

Each characteristic is associated with a specific trade off. A flat structure, for example, allows faster communication between the different levels, but it will require a wider span of control. The decentralization of decisions can lower bureaucratic costs and contributes to a better coordination of the activities, though it can overload the Project Manager with information, causing a delay in the project.

The <u>Functional Structure</u> splits the members of the project into teams according to their specialty (e.g., similar skills, tools, or techniques). The Housekeeping Project under this structure would probably have one team specialize in each of the 5Ss. One team would be responsible for cleaning, the other for health, and so on. It would be a less flexible structure, but due to their specialization, they would be able to generate faster results with great quality.

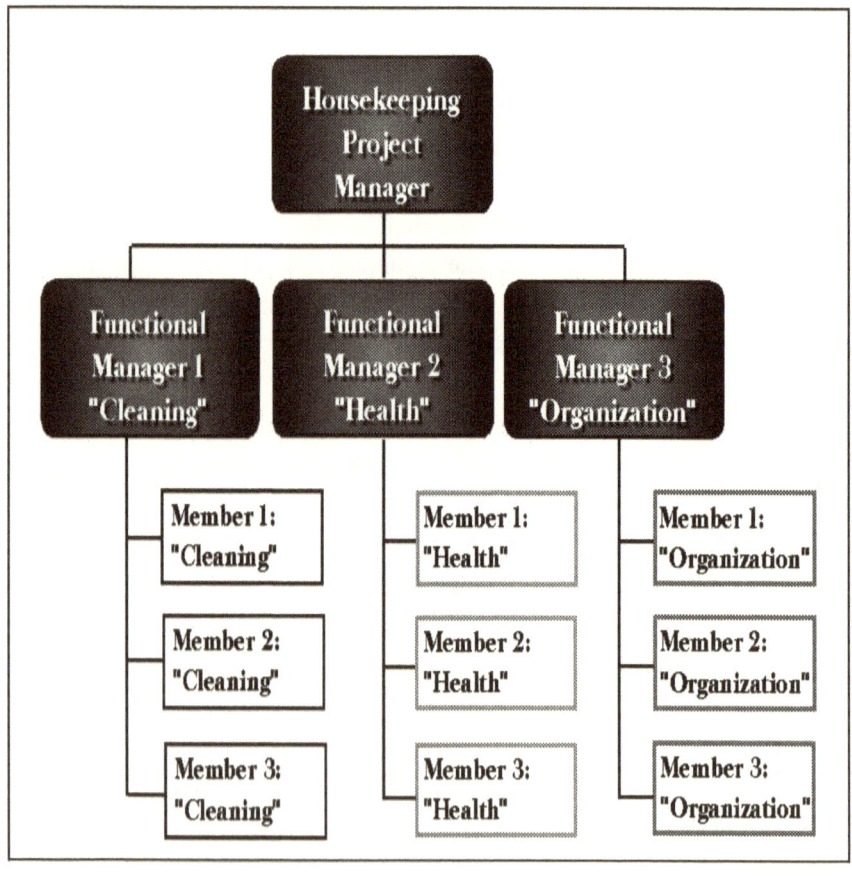

Figure 5: Example of Functional Structure for a Housekeeping Project

The Product Structure brings together people with distinct skills. The combined abilities of the members of the team are responsible for the development of a full product. In the Housekeeping Project, the Project Manager used this structure. He put together people with different backgrounds with the common goal of improving their departments. This could only be obtained with the combined efforts of everyone in the team. Note that different backgrounds don't necessarily mean different departments. This is a flexible structure since the multifunctional team is able to deal with a great variety of problems and embrace wide scopes.

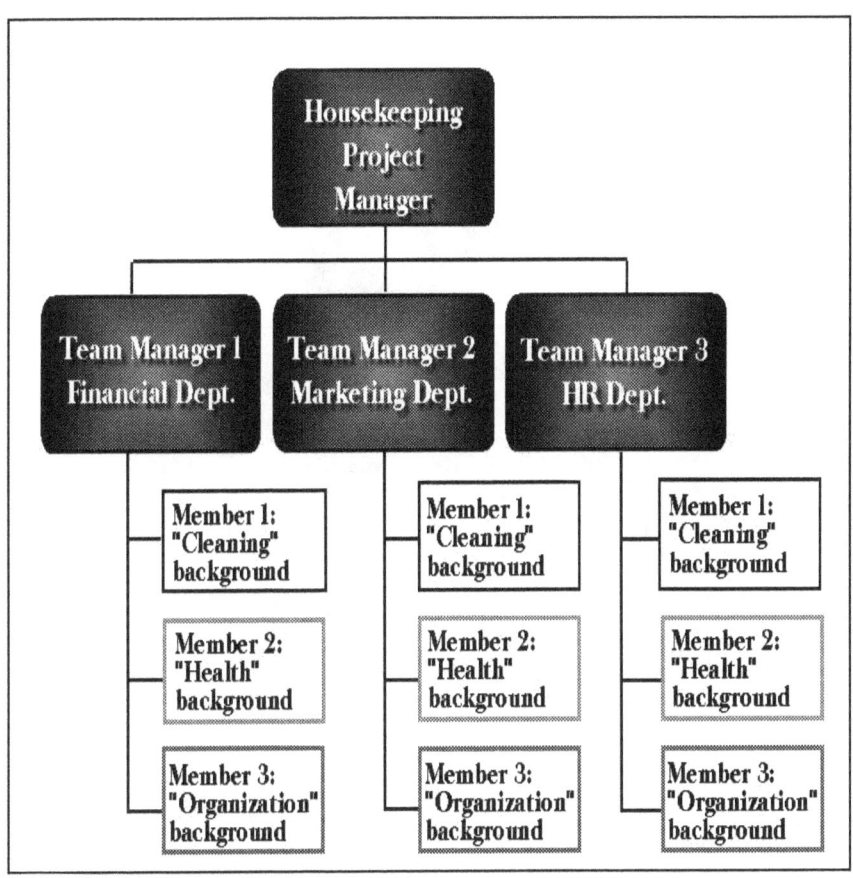

Figure 6: Example of Product Structure for a Housekeeping Project

The <u>Matrix Structure</u> is a mix of the Function and Product. Though it is very flexible, it has a complex network of relationships. Each team member is allocated to a team just like in the Product Structure. However, the team member also belongs to a Functional Structure. In other words, in the Housekeeping Project, we would have a specific team member from each department answering for one of the 5Ss. For example, the specialists in the activities associated with health would share their experiences and best practices with each other and take this knowledge back to their team in a coordinated action. The product team leader would evaluate and negotiate the strategy of implementation of that particular solution with the functional team leader. As we can see, one of the problems with this structure is the existence of two leaders for each team member, which can be a potential cause of problems.

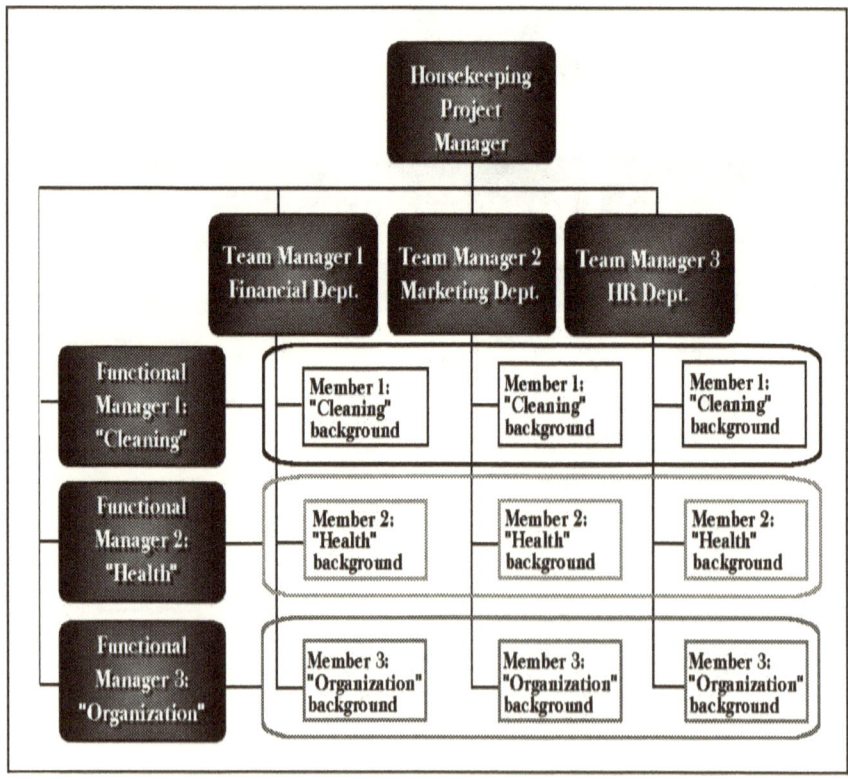

Figure 7: Example of Matrix Structure for a Housekeeping Project

To improve the integration in the organization structure, the Project Manager can use several tools, such as direct contact with team members, the creation of liaison roles in each team, the development of cross-functional teams and committees to deal with specific issues, and others.

We shouldn't forget to include in our project organizational structure the figure of the Steering Committee. This group will be the ultimate approver of the decisions, results, and strategies used by the Project Manager. The Steering Committee will dictate the guidelines for the scope and objectives of the project. They should show commitment and support towards the project and the Project Manager.

After defining the organizational structure of the project, it is important to define the communication strategy. The project team needs mechanisms to communicate within the team and outside of it, with the stakeholders.

The internal communication plan creates procedures to ensure fast and reliable communication. We may define the rules for meetings (e.g., frequency and participants who should attend), how to communicate an issue (e.g., e-mail to the manager or to the owner of the issue, use of issues database, and meetings), and how to keep everyone informed of the progress of each team.

Sometimes, some people in a company hosting the project won't be willing to accept changes. Therefore, we should plan ahead the best way to communicate the benefits of the changes and involve them in the activities as much as possible. This external communication plan is also part of a change management strategy.

In fact, the first step in our change management strategy is the identification of the stakeholders, which is an activity developed in the very beginning of the project.

Based on the expectations and characteristics of each person or department, the Project Manager designs a specific communication plan and keeps track of the acceptance of the project and changes in expectations along the whole project. Some of the most common tools available for the Project Manager are newsletters, workshops, social events, project website, contests, surveys, and interviews. These tools may look simple, but they can be very powerful if applied in the correct way.

A survey may use advanced statistical analyses, including regressions, factor analyses, and other techniques to identify the correct preference of a specific group and verify that all the important factors were taken into consideration. In the third part of this book, we show how some statistical tools can be used to help the project management to analyze the opinions of the customers.

We saw in the Housekeeping Project how the Project Manager utilized a contest in order to change the mentality of the employees. First, he introduced the concepts of 5S. Then, he proposed a contest that would make people think about the meaning and benefits of the project.

To represent the Housekeeping Project through a draw, the employees would first have to understand the 5S philosophy and assimilate at least part of that. After understanding a new concept, people are more willing to accept and embrace it.

4.7 - Project Charter

Basically, the Project Charter is a compilation of all the information of the preparation phase. It will serve as a guide and a contract between the Project Manager and the stakeholders. It should contain all the assumptions and agreements between the Project Manager and the sponsor of the project.

The Project Charter describes the history and goals of the project, as well as the critical factors of success. It defines the scope, risk assessment, implementation strategy, detailed schedule, necessary resources, organizational structure, human resources management plan, documentation strategy, project budget, and change management strategy.

The description of the activities and scope in the Project Charter is also called a Statement of Work (SOW). This statement has to be reviewed and updated every time we have a change in the parameters of the project.

If we are talking about a project in a company other than the Project Manager's, the Project Charter may also include a brief description of the industry, company, and main products as a quick reference for any external resource.

In the ERP project, for example, the project proposal presented by the consulting firm included a description of the client and its industry segment. This was made in order to demonstrate that they had the correct understanding of their business.

At this point, the Project Charter may be considered a very advanced draft. Although the Project Manager has tried to work with the stakeholders and sponsors of the project, the whole content of the Project Charter may change before it is signed by the sponsors. The Project Manager should take this opportunity to review all the details of the project and adjust any numbers.

Some projects have their scope, implementation strategy, resources, and other points changed during the course of their development. These changes should be negotiated with the sponsors, the impacts should be evaluated, and the Project Charter changed accordingly.

Of course, all these documents will generate a thick Project Charter. In order to help the readers to have a quick understanding of the project, it is advisable to create an Executive Summary, a one- to two-page document containing a concise definition of the project, goals, scope, team, and main deadlines. A good example is the Six-Sigma Project Charter adopted by some companies, presented in the third part of the book. In a glance, we are able to describe the project and know whom to contact in case of any questions.

The Project Charter helps the Project Manager to sell the project to the sponsors. He has to clearly articulate the benefits of the project in a way that is compelling to each sponsor. The Project Charter will bring all the rationale with concrete numbers, which can be negotiated using clear and realistic criteria.

In the ERP project, David, the Project Manager, didn't have all the costs or the detailed schedule until the first week of the development phase. However, he set the conclusion of the Project Charter as a top priority.

Sometimes, we don't have all the components in place to finish the Project Charter before the project execution is authorized. The Project Manager has to work toward the completion of this document and get it approved by the Steering Committee to protect both parts from a misunderstanding in terms of scope, work method, and schedule.

5 – Project Execution

The Execution Phase is also known as "Development," "Engagement," and "Implementation." In this phase, the Project Manager makes sure that all the activities defined in the Project Schedule are implemented as defined in the Project Charter. Time, cost, and quality are some of the main concerns of the Project Manager in this phase.

As we said before, each project will have a different approach to solving specific problems, reaching specific goals. Therefore, the activities in this phase change a lot from one project to another. However, for a general case, we may define the following steps during the Execution Phase:

- ✓ Kick-off Meeting
- ✓ Project Team Training
- ✓ Execution of Activities
- ✓ Execution of Change Management
- ✓ Solution Test
- ✓ Customer Training
- ✓ Quality Check

Once more, we have to remember that the length of each step depends on the nature and size of the project. Furthermore, as in the Preparation Phase, we will see several activities associated with Integration, Quality, Risk Management, Communication, Scope, Cost, and Time Management in each step of the Execution Phase.

Sometimes the Project Manager is responsible for coordinating all the execution activities, such as in the Housekeeping and New Product Development projects. However, he may delegate part of the coordination responsibilities to other managers, such as in the ERP Implementation Project. The Project Manager of that project had some other managers coordinating the Integration, IT, Change Management, and other activities.

Nevertheless, he has to remember that no matter how many people he has helping in the coordination of the activities, the Project Manager is always the one ultimately responsible for the project.

5.1 - Kick-off Meeting

The kick-off meeting is the activity transitioning between the Preparation and Execution Phases. The kick-off may have different formats depending on the goals and nature of the project. We may have a simple meeting, a workshop, a cocktail, a dinner, a week with meetings in a hotel, or any other format. Each format allows for a different level of interaction between the participants and a different way to convey the messages from the presenter.

The first task is to define the goals of the meeting. The most usual goals are:

- the introduction of the project;
- achieving the support of sponsors and key stakeholders;
- defining roles and responsibilities;
- and team building.

The audience should include key stakeholders, project members, and sponsors of the project. The project should be introduced to them in a very didactic way. The goals of the project should be presented if possible, making reference to the areas of the stakeholders.

The audience should be able to see the benefits of the project for the organization and for their particular area. Every interaction with a stakeholder is an opportunity to sell the project and to ensure his support and commitment.

Usually, many of the participants don't know how the project intends to reach the presented goals. Therefore, it is important to give them a brief explanation of the Work Plan highlighting the main activities and dates. If we are talking about the introduction of a new technology or work method, a quick theory should also be part of the presentation.

In an ERP project, for example, it is a good idea to explain what an ERP is, including its main functionalities, and offer a brief introduction of the main players in the market providing this kind of system or, more specifically, the vendor who will provide the ERP being implemented. In a Housekeeping Project following the 5S Philosophy, it is necessary to explain the main concepts behind this philosophy and to show some examples of achievements from companies who have implemented similar projects.

This presentation should also cover the project organizational structure, implementation strategy, scope, and any other information that would allow the team members to identify their roles and responsibilities.

It is highly recommended to have the sponsors of the project say some words about the importance of the project. They should make clear the priority of that initiative and show their full support through motivational speeches. Whenever possible, they should give proof of this commitment by asking their subordinates about the status of the project, attending events, and serving as examples and role models.

The execution of many projects starts right after the kick-off meeting. Therefore, the team should create a bond as fast as possible. The stronger the bond between the team members, the faster and smoother their decisions will be. Consequently, some ice-breaker and team building activities are recommended in order to give a jump start to the interpersonal relationships among the project members.

5.2 - Project Team Training

During this step, the teams receive the knowledge needed to perform their tasks. Generally, the volume of training required by a project member is superior to the volume of training required by the final customer of the project. The team members are usually trained to implement the project, deliver it, and to maintain the solution after it has been implemented. However, they may not need to acquire all the knowledge at once. Therefore, several training sessions covering different topics may be scheduled along the course of the project.

The initial training shouldn't cover only the technical aspects of the project, such as the 5S Philosophy in the Housekeeping Project and the ERP functionalities in the ERP Implementation. The initial training should also prepare the team to communicate within the project, present the documentation strategy and tools, reinforce the project schedule, and highlight the main deliverables of each activity.

The Project Manager should remember to verify the location of the training, instructor, dates, and necessary material. These items should have already been described in the Human Resources Management Plan created in the Preparation Phase of the project.

The training format will vary according to the needs of the project. It may be a traditional presentation, an interactive workshop, a debate, on-the-job training, or computer-based training. Each one has its advantages and disadvantages and should be evaluated by the Project Manager to see if the one chosen fits the project purpose and can be effective in transitioning the necessary knowledge to the attendants.

5.3 - Work Plan Execution

During the work plan execution, the team members develop the activities defined in the first phase of the project while the Project Manager supports their work and copes with many other issues.

One of the roles of the Project Manager in this phase is to control the financials of the project. He must have a procedure in place to correctly organize the billings and collections of the project. In some projects, it is possible to use the Accounts Payable and Accounts Receivable

Departments of the company to perform this job. However, the Project Manager should have a way to differentiate the expenses of the project from the others of the company. The creation of one or more cost centers, or any other cost collector, may be helpful. The Project Manager should also analyze if the existing charging codes are detailed enough to assure an accurate representation of the expenses and facilitate tracking procedures.

In the ERP Project, we saw that David, the Project Manager from the consulting company, had periodic meetings with the client's Project Manager in order to discuss the financials of the project. They discussed not only the invoices from the vendors but also the invoices for the consulting services, the status of the project budget, the financial forecast, and any issue related to unexpected expenses.

David was the liaison between the client and the consulting firm. Therefore, he would have to supply the necessary explanations for any billing document for the consulting services.

The forms chosen to handle budget concerns may vary from case to case. Usually, in an ERP implementation, the client's Project Manager is responsible for part of the budget of the project, and the consulting Project Manager is responsible for the other part. Therefore, we usually have a great interaction between the managers to discuss their interpretation of the contract and their responsibilities to the budget. During the financial meetings, they have to agree on the procedures regarding budget management, scope control, and contract changes. All these items are part of the assumptions used to set the budget. Consequently, it is critical that the project management team understand these assumptions and their impact if they are not met.

The creation of a contingency fund is also advisable in long projects and for those with an unstable environment where definitions, procedures, and needs change with a certain frequency. Although this fund may be available, the Project Manager should remember that his goal is to finish the project under budget. This additional budget should be available up front to avoid negotiation rounds with the Steering Committee to request additional funding during the project. This may shift the attention of the Project Manager from other important project issues.

Another concern of the Project Manager during this phase is the progress of each team. The Project Manager should identify bottlenecks and reasons for delays. Then, he has to work close to the teams creating options to get the activities back on the original schedule, with the desired productivity level.

The Project Manager has an active role in promoting integration. He has to be sure that the interaction among the teams is at a satisfactory level and that people are sharing their knowledge and supporting one another. Furthermore, he has to ensure that the transitions between activities and phases are running smoothly, with no unresolved issues or gaps.

The satisfaction of the staff is also a constant concern of the Project Manager. He has to ensure that the team members are comfortable with their roles and the opportunities offered to them. To accomplish that, the Project Manager has to align their expectations with the roles they are assigned on the project. Following that, the manager can monitor the performance of the staff based on the pre-defined criteria.

Constant feedback is always a good way to keep everyone's expectations on track. If a mismatch between the expectation of a team member and his role in the project is identified, this divergence should be fixed immediately. If no agreement is reached, the Project Manager should consider replacing that resource, especially if they are in the beginning of the project where transitions and substitutions are more manageable and the impact on the team's morale is not so big.

During this phase, a lot of new problems may show up, and the Project Manager may have to make many adjustments to the work plan. However, the Project Manager must have his focus on the scope of the project. He has to keep the boundaries of the project as intact as possible in order to avoid delays in the project.

In the Housekeeping Project, that would mean not to include new branches or goals into the original project. In the ERP implementation, that would mean not to include additional modules, interfaces, processes, technical enhancements, reports, data conversions and organizational units (e.g. subsidiary). In the New Product Development Project, that would mean avoiding the addition of other product segments than athletic shoes.

To achieve this goal, the Project Manager has to communicate the scope to all levels of the organization and explain the consequences of an unplanned scope change. It may have a strong impact on timing requirements, budget, and consequently on the project bonus. Nevertheless, if the scope has to change, the Project Manager must document all the changes and impacts with a cost benefit analysis. The Steering Committee usually has to authorize changes in the scope of the project. In addition, the Project Manager should communicate the changes throughout the organization.

The Project Manager has to maintain good communication with the Steering Committee. He has to keep them informed of the status of the project in order to anticipate any problems as early as possible. A status report should be issued periodically by the Project Manager, including major activities in progress, concluded tasks, and planned activities for the next period. A high-level schedule highlighting main changes is also a good way to inform others. Furthermore, the report should include any findings or preliminary observations, critical issues and concerns, scope changes, and changes in the resources plan.

Another task for the Project Manager during this phase is to control the risk of the activities and project as a whole. In order to do that, the Project Manager uses the risk analysis spreadsheet he developed in the initial phase of the project. He has to update the risk assessment table and keep track of the activities with higher risks.

The Project Manager also has an active role to evaluate the quality of the documentation generated by the teams. They need to be complete, easy to understand, and follow the pre-defined templates. Quick audits to check the documents from each team are advisable.

Finally, the Project Manager has to execute the issue resolution process previously defined. This process helps to document and correct major issues that may be raised during the implementation. The issue resolution process should be used to treat any problem that occurs that can't be solved by the project team or that require upper management or additional expertise to resolve.

The tool used to manage the issues should allow access to every team leader. Therefore, two or more teams won't be registering the same issue. Furthermore, they may find another team with a similar issue and leverage on their experience. The database with the identified problems during the project may be used as reference in future projects.

The issues should be evaluated and prioritized according to their impact on the schedule, the quality of the project, complexity, and other criteria that the Project Manager deems appropriate for the specific project. The issue should be explained in as much detail as possible, including information such as the background of the problem, scope, and impacts. The solution description should bring the alternative solutions proposed, rationale for a specific recommendation, and estimates of resources for the correction. Any issue that cannot be solved by the Project Manager should be redirected to the Steering Committee with all the necessary information to support their decision process.

5.4 - Change Management Execution

There are many change management activities to be developed during the project. It is not easy to change the way people behave and make them more willing to accept all the changes a project brings. Therefore, these activities are extremely important for the success of the project.

Communication is the main tool the Project Manager has to make people change. He makes a constant effort to show everyone the benefits of the project and all the changes. His mission is to make people not just comfortable with the changes but also willing to help and embrace them. Therefore, he has to guarantee that the project will have a two-way communication channel with sponsors, stakeholders, and project teams.

The Project Manager has to constantly assess the impacts of the project on the organization and individuals. He should talk to the team members to understand these impacts and to determine the best way to minimize those that may be negative. Whenever possible, the Project Manager tries to involve the stakeholders of the main impacted areas in the decisions and strategies to sell the project to their teams. This may create a sense of ownership of the project that will greatly help in the acceptance of all the changes.

Motivation is one of the keys to achieving productivity and quality. Therefore, the Project Manager has to execute the motivation plan developed in the Preparation Phase and evaluate its results.

Sometimes, the Project Manager won't be able to reach all the stakeholders using a general strategy. If after using all the communication and motivational tools he misses the acceptance of one or more important stakeholders, he has to create a personalized action plan to reach each individual. He has to study their roles in the organization, behaviors, and psychographics to find out the most appealing method to convince them of the benefits of the project and to get their support.

Some change management tools are very similar to marketing tools. In both cases, we try to make someone adopt a product or philosophy. Therefore, we may observe similar stages in his acceptance process. Some marketing specialists use the AIDA model to characterize these stages. AIDA stands for Awareness, Interest, Desire, and Adoption.

In the Awareness Stage, we transmit the knowledge to the customer, so he can understand what the product is, where to find it, and other characteristics. In the Interest Stage, we try to motivate the customer to adopt the new product, showing all the benefits. In the Desire Stage, we reinforce the conviction of the customer and try to help him transform his motivation into a real action. Finally, the Adoption Stage is defined by the acquisition and use of the product.

In change management work, the customer goes through similar stages, understanding the changes, its benefits, and transforming his understanding into real actions supporting the changing initiatives until the adoption of the new procedures. At the end, the customers should have different behaviors and attitudes.

5.5 - Solution Test

Depending on the nature of the project, we may have several kinds of solution tests in order to ensure the quality of the results. The Project Manager should invite key stakeholders and sponsors for the main tests. These invitees evaluate the results, align their expectations, and show their support and commitment to the project. Once more, the Project Manager has the opportunity to highlight the benefits and main changes brought by the project in order to create a favorable environment for everyone to accept the changes.

Testing a complex solution is not easy. The Project Manager may have to divide the tests into many pieces. Some of the most popular subdivisions for the tests are:

- *Component test* – one single component or functionality of the project is tested. In a project where a machine is built, we may exemplify this kind of test as the evaluation of a single lamp, which is part of the machine. For a system implementation, we may think about a particular feature of the system. For example, we may verify whether the system is correctly calculating the depreciation for a specific asset.

- *Scenario test* – a process with specific parameters is tested. In a system implementation, it would represent a specific process, such as paying an invoice. The idea is to test a group of functionalities necessary to execute a specific process. In a project where a machine is built, we might associate this kind of test with the test of a specific part of the equipment. For example, we might be_testing only the electrical or hydraulic part of a machine.

- *Integrated test* – a sequence of complex cross-functional processes are tested. This is one of the most difficult tests. In a system implementation project, we would be analyzing the interaction between different areas of the system. We may think in a complete scenario starting with the creation of a purchase request, going through the vendor evaluation, quotes, the creation of a purchase order, goods receipt, payment of invoice, creation of the asset, depreciation, and sale of the asset. In a project where we build a machine, it would be the test of all functionalities of the machine.

- *Stress test* – the bottlenecks of the new components, sequences, or activities resulting from the project are tested under unfavorable conditions in order to evaluate the behavior of the project output in peak hours. In a system implementation, these tests relate to the slowest processes in the system, such as running an MRP or depreciation. This helps to verify whether the hardware was properly dimensioned, or if an upgrade or some sort of adjustment in the database is necessary. For a project where a machine is built, it would mean running the machine under unfavorable conditions, such as for long hours, in high humidity, in a dusty environment, or under high temperatures in order to evaluate whether the machine will be able to perform as required, even in a hostile environment.

- *Security test* – it tests the access of unauthorized people to the components of the equipment/system/processes. The reliability of the solution may depend on the premise that the equipment/system/processes will remain with the characteristics delivered at the end of the project. Therefore, some authorization measures should be put in place to avoid alterations in the configuration of the system, the components of the equipment, or the final documentation of the processes.

- *Field test* – the solution of the project is tested under conditions representing the environment where the solution will be applied. The goal of this test is to analyze the interaction of the solution with the end users and the environment where it will be used. Characteristics like safety, usability, adaptation, efficiency, efficacy, and others are evaluated in this test.

The Project Manager should plan the tests according to the needs and characteristics of the project. He should invite the necessary people and when applicable, prepare a guide with the features being tested and the expected outcome in order to help the evaluators. After the tests, a summary of the main results should be communicated to the sponsors and stakeholders.

5.6 – Customer Training

Some of the projects have to deliver not only new equipment or systems but also knowledge from the project team to the customer. This knowledge is required to maintain the project alive after it is delivered.

The customer should be trained to operate the new system, use the new machine, execute the new process, run the new analyses and deal with eventual problems that might happen.

The Project Manager ensures that the project team prepares the manual of operations to help the customer to operate the new machine/system or run the new processes. The customer training should cover the manual of operations and help the customer with any questions he may have.

The Project Manager also decides on the best format for the training. It may be on-the-job training, case analyses, lectures, simulations, or any other way with a better fit to the project and customer.

After the training sessions, the customer should fill out a training program evaluation form in order to highlight any problems, talk about uncovered points, and suggest improvements. The Project Manager may answer to some of the comments by offering complementary training and making any necessary adjustments to the course structure.

5.7 - Quality Check Points

Many projects usually have a very tight schedule. Consequently, the pressure for results may cause the project members to lose focus on quality. Quality checkpoints are used to evaluate the achievements to date and to ensure that they correspond to the expected level of quality.

It is recommended to have a quality checkpoint after each important activity. The Project Manager defines the structure of these quality checks. It may be a single interview with the team leaders and key stakeholders, a technical assessment of the project, or a checklist with the outputs of each activity.

Whenever it is possible, the evaluation should be conducted by an outside expert. After evaluating the work of the project teams, the evaluator should write a quality check report with the status of the evaluated activities. The expert should highlight the main problems, identify threats to the project, and suggest possible courses of action. The quality check should be clear in terms of deliverables expected and should then describe what was observed.

The Project Manager should inform the Steering Committee, key stakeholders, and project team of the results of each quality check. The successes should be celebrated to maintain good momentum.

Since the results of the quality check may be unfavorable, the Project Manager should be ready to deal with failures. He must have a back-up plan and be ready to negotiate changes in the project with the Steering Committee. Depending on the problem, he may try to get additional resources, change the scope, or get a time extension to conclude the project.

6 – Project Delivery

The Project Delivery Phase is also known as the "Closing," or "Final" phase. In this phase, the Project Manager finalizes all of the activities and evaluates the success of the project. He acknowledges that everything was delivered as specified in the Project Charter and that the sponsors and key stakeholders are satisfied with the results.

The most common activities in this phase are:

- ✓ Assisted Operation
- ✓ Operation Support
- ✓ Implementation Review
- ✓ Executive Presentation
- ✓ Team Evaluation
- ✓ Project Celebration

6.1 – Assisted Operation

As we said before, the Project Manager chooses between different solutions and implementation strategies. The assisted operation is the moment the equipment, process, or system actually starts to work in the real environment. This is a critical period, which requires the attention of the full project team. They usually follow the customer in the first few steps of the operation to ensure that the knowledge was successfully transferred. The customer must know not only how to operate the new equipment or system but also when to use each different feature and how to take full advantage of the product to increase productivity.

The Project Manager should have a contingency plan ready to put in place in case any failure is noticed during the assisted operation. He should be focusing on the collection of the metrics to analyze the effectiveness of the project.

For example, considering an ERP implementation, the Project Manager would try to collect feedback from the areas in the first day of operation and verify whether the company was able to maintain its normal operations. If something goes wrong with a specific part of the ERP, the manager has to analyze the possibility of fixing the problem, deactivate the specific functionality that is not working, and use a manual procedure while the problem is being fixed. In a very extreme case, he analyzes a strategy to turn off the ERP and go back to the legacy system.

If the project goal is to build an industrial oven, the first few days of the oven will require the constant attention of the Project Manager and his team. They will try to collect several measurements such as temperature, fuel consumption, and the color of the bricks. If problems are detected, the Project Manager should get more information and decide whether to implement the contingency plan or not.

6.2 – Operation Support

After the assisted operation, the client starts to work alone with the new process, equipment, or system. However, he may encounter some problems beyond his knowledge or capacity to solve. Therefore, there should be a help desk structure ready to support him.

The Project Manager helps the customer to identify the best way to fit the help desk into the structure of the organization. Depending on the size of the project and the necessary level of support, we may have a decentralized structure with specialists and process owners allocated in different departments.

The Help Desk may also be centralized in a single department with a dedicated staff or not. The dedicated staff would only answer questions regarding the process, equipment, or system implemented during the project. The non-dedicated staff would have a broader scope, answering questions related to other areas or projects, too. In the ERP implementation for example, we may have a department responsible for answering only questions related to the ERP. On the other hand, we may have a department answering the ERP questions and any other problem related to IT.

We may also think about having a multi-level help-desk structure. For example, the first level of contact after a problem has been detected should be directed to a local specialist, maybe in the department of the customer. He would try to help and, depending on the complexity of the problem, he would forward it to a higher support level, perhaps the national support, and so on. In theory, this structure would prevent small problems and simple questions from overloading top specialists. Let's keep in mind that sometimes we may also outsource the support. We may have an internal first support level and an outsourced second support level.

After deciding on the structure and layers of support, we should consider the communication channels the customer can use to reach support. These channels also vary according to the company and project. The different channels may go from a simple phone call or walk-in to remote support on the web.

Finally, the support plan should be communicated to everybody in the organization. The Project Manager should advise the client to continuously measure the efficiency and effectiveness of the Help Desk. The Project Manager may also suggest some indicators to keep track of the Help Desk performance.

6.3 – Implementation Review

This is the moment where we take one step back to analyze the results of the project. In many projects, we will see immediate results, but most of the time, the results may take days, weeks, months, or even years. Therefore, the Project Manager should prepare a report with the immediate results and a plan to measure the upcoming benefits of the project. In fact, the result analysis should already have been included in the Project Schedule.

During the implementation review, the Project Manager should double check the financials of the project and be sure that he accounted for every expense made. A short summary of the final financial situation of the project should be added to the final implementation review document.

The Project Manager should also ensure that no troubleshooting issues have remained opened. All problems should have already been addressed. He should also consider including in the final document a brief assessment of the training program, of the communication strategy implementation, and of any other item responsible for a big impact on the project.

As we can see, the first part of the Implementation Review Report is dedicated to analyzing the project development, the main outputs of the project, and the immediate results. The remainder of the report should include recommendations for the future.

The Project Manager should also be sure to destroy or turn back any confidential document utilized or created during the project. The remaining document should be organized and filed in the appropriate way (CD, hard copies, etc.) for future reference. He should remember that every project is a learning opportunity, and a good Project Manager knows how to leverage his knowledge using his past experiences.

Based on the results of the project, surveys, feedbacks, formal and informal conversations, and other available sources, the Project Manager may use a SWOT diagram to present the strengths, weaknesses, opportunities, and threats of the project.

As a result, the Project Manager may suggest improvements on the current system, process, or equipment, or the development of a new project with the same characteristics in order to rollout the solution to other areas, departments, companies, or geographic sites.

Since the improvement suggestions are usually results of high-level analyses, they should be used by the readers only as a guide. Because the suggestions can generate other projects, the Project Manager should go back to the Project Preparation Phase in case the client demonstrates additional interest.

An executive summary of the final report should also be prepared. In this one to two-page document, the Project Manager should highlight the main achievements of the project and make suggestions for future developments.

6.4 – Executive Presentation

The executive presentation is the formal closing of the project. It is designed to effectively transfer the knowledge and results from the project team to the client. The Steering Committee and sponsors of the project should be present in this meeting.

In this phase, the Project Manager uses the Project Chart and the Implementation Review Report to show the achieved goals and an overview of the project development. If the communication with the sponsors and key stakeholders was effective during the project, the information presented here shouldn't be a surprise for anyone.

Besides the overall balance of the project, the Project Manager should also present suggestions for improvement, such as upgrades, rollouts, and changes in the project, as described in the Implementation Review Report.

Finally, he should take the opportunity to answer any questions the sponsors might have and to verify that their expectations have been completely fulfilled.

6.5 – Team Evaluation

During the Delivery Phase, the Project Manager has to close the evaluations of the team members. A fair evaluation will help in the selection process for future projects. Besides, it may serve as a guide for the personal development of the individual being evaluated, since it will highlight not only their strengths but also points to be developed. Therefore, it must be as accurate as possible.

One of the most common problems with evaluations is the subjectivity of the process. The Project Manager has to be fair and avoid evaluating the team members based on his personal impressions, feelings, and opinions. As much as possible, he has to use quantitative data and tangible examples of the attitudes and achievements of the professionals being evaluated.

Most managers are used to evaluating their employees based only on financial performance. To minimize this problem, some companies started using a tool called Balanced Scorecard. This tool has been growing in popularity in the last few years. It complements the financial performance criteria with three additional perspectives: customers, business processes, and learning & growth.

The Balanced Scorecard helps the company/project to focus on results and to build capabilities for the future. This is important not only for the Project Manager, who may work with the same team in future projects, but also for the employees who seek self and professional development.

Kaplan and Norton [17] state that the Balanced Scorecard is a tool that can be used to translate the vision and strategies of a company into action. The same idea can be used in a project. The Project Manager has to translate the vision of the stakeholders and project strategy into actions and link that to the different areas of the Balanced Scorecard (financial performance, customer focus, business process excellence, and learning & growth).

For each area of the Balanced Scorecard, the Project Manager has to define goals using the same philosophy he applied while creating the project goals. It means that he should use SMART goals (Specific, Measurable, Achievable, Realistic, and with a Time component). These goals should be reviewed and adjusted during the many feedback meetings that occur during the course of the project between the Project Manager and the employee.

6.6 - Project Celebration

It is important to celebrate each successful project with a social gathering. This is the informal event that marks the conclusion of the project. Here, the Project Manager may communicate the main results reached and recognize the efforts of all those involved.

During the project, the Project Manager has worked to make the project team feel responsible for the project. Since most of them should have developed a feeling of ownership, it is fair to let them know what they achieved by sharing high-level information about the results of the project. This attitude will make them proud and motivate them for future projects.

The sponsors and key stakeholders should also be present in the celebration. Although the project is over, their presence shows the importance of the project for the organization and reinforces the need for taking full advantage of the output of the project (e.g., equipment, processes, and systems).

PART III

Tools for Project Management

7 – Basic Tools

There are many tools available to help the Project Manager plan, run, and evaluate the project. The tools are not a requirement for any particular project, but they can be used to speed up the activities, ensure the quality of the outputs of each phase, support the conclusions of some analyses, and prioritize issues.

In this book, we show some tools that can be used in most of the projects. Some of them are considered basic and very straightforward. Others are complex but very useful.

We don't intend to transmit the complete knowledge of any specific tool. Our goal is to give an overview of some tools and motivate the reader to look for further information and learn more about them. A good Project Manager develops the capability of learning, combining, and creating new approaches and uses for the available tools.

In this chapter, we present some basic tools. These tools are simple tables or diagrams that help the Project Manager during evaluations, planning activities, and analyses.

7.1 - Communication

Communication is not a tool, but it is the most important skill a Project Manager has. In fact, it is so important that I want to remind the reader how necessary this skill is in any situation.

How many times in a project do we use some kind of communication? We do it all the time. Every time we try to transmit a message or someone tries to tell us something, we are communicating.

Someone may think that if he can speak clearly and listen carefully, he will have no problems communicating. However, communication is more than words. The sender may choose many different ways to transmit a message.

A message can be written in an e-mail, on a piece of paper or white board, sent via fax, or forwarded through various other means. For each of them, we may see different styles and rules applying to the format and structure.

A message can also be transmitted in a wordless way through gestures and symbols. Many books show how to interpret specific gestures. A simple example of a symbol is the clothes someone wears. Most people use a number of symbols when they go out on dates. They try to wear nice clothes and go to beautiful places with the right illumination, music, and scent in order to better transmit a romantic message.

Wainright [25] shows how important body language is in the communication process.

Let's try a quick exercise. Figure 8 presents the first symbols of a logical sequence. Try to guess the next symbols of the sequence.

Figure 8: First four terms of a logical sequence

A sequence we try to decode is like a message that we can't understand. Maybe you already know the next term of the sequence, maybe not. The first time I saw this sequence was in college. My teacher in the engineering school presented it to a class with 100 students. Only three were able to understand this sequence after only four symbols.

Try to describe the second and fourth terms of the sequence. Most people would say they look like an underlined heart and the letter "M" crossed. They describe these terms in this way because of previous knowledge — because this is a pattern they are used to seeing.

Our perception of a message is based on our knowledge and previous experiences. Sometimes, these things block us from seeing the true meaning of a message.

In a project, we may have people with different backgrounds and cultures. These differences make each one understand and transmit a message in a different way.

Let's try to add some other symbols to our logical sequence and see if it gets easier. Figure 9 shows the first seven terms of the sequence.

Figure 9: First seven terms of a logical sequence

Did it help? Try to break the symbols into different pieces. Try not to see what you're used to seeing. Don't think there is a heart in the second symbol or a letter "M" in the fourth. In fact, maybe the message is not about geometrical forms such as circles and triangles. Don't see just the things you believe, and don't believe in what you are seeing. When you don't understand something, you should try to analyze the message in a different way.

In projects, we receive a lot of messages, and if we don't understand the idea the sender is trying to transmit, we may make the wrong decisions.

The symbols are symmetrical for a reason. This sequence is called numbers in a mirror. The right side of the figure is only a number, and the left is its reflection in a mirror.

This exercise was only to highlight how important communication is for a Project Manager and to warn that he must have an open mind to understand and transmit any message.

Once more, we highlight that communication is a two-way process and may be done in many different ways. Since people tend to decode the messages based on their personal experiences and knowledge, the more a Project Manager knows his team, the easier and better the communication will be. That is one of the reasons why team building activities and social gatherings are so important.

7.2 – Stakeholder Perception Map

A good relationship with the stakeholders is a critical factor of success in any project. Unfortunately, there is no magic way to help the Project Manager with this task. To achieve a good level of integration with the stakeholders, the Project Manager depends a lot on his charisma and sales skills. Every contact with the stakeholder is an opportunity to sell the project.

I don't intend to talk about sales and negotiation techniques, though I strongly recommend to every Project Manager to try to learn more about these topics since they are important in every project. However, allow me to make an observation about some common points I saw in a few outstanding salespeople.

Good salespeople are usually excellent communicators and have great empathy. They use these abilities to understand more about their customers, find out what they want, and show them how their product fits their requirements.

A Stakeholder Perception Map has a similar philosophy. It tries to help the Project Manager to evaluate, understand, verify the expectations, prioritize, and manage the relationship with the different stakeholders.

It is basically a table maintained by the Project Manager to support the change management activities during the course of the project. The Project Manager periodically updates this table with the input of his team.

The example in Figure 10 has only five stakeholders and some standard columns. However, let's remember that a Project Manager should have creativity as one of his greatest resources. Therefore, he may modify the table to attend to the specific needs of the project.

Usually, this kind of map has columns identifying the key stakeholders, the nature of their involvement with the project, their main issues and goals. The responsible for contacting each stakeholder may help the Project Manager to link the stakeholder goals to the objectives of the project.

As we can see in the example in Figure 11, the first few columns identify the stakeholder and his role in the project. His importance is also considered. The relative importance is a subjective criterion, which tries to evaluate the impact a disagreement with that stakeholder would have on the project. This column helps the Project Manager to establish priorities while managing relationships.

STAKEHOLDER PERCEPTION MAP

#	Stakeholder	Area	Relative Importance (1.10)	Nature of Involvement	Key Issues	Perceptions	Observations	Objectives	Constraints	Overall Readiness for Change (1.10)	Actions	Responsible	Status
1	Mr. Elkin Lopezmaio	Logistics	6	Logistics Analyst - He is the main contact with the companies and carriers. He will be the liaison between the project and the carriers	We will need his collaboration to implement the new relationship system with carriers	He thinks the project is a good teaming and improvement opportunity	Good technical skills. Detailed oriented person	His performance is measured on Cost improvements. On time deliveries and other logistics ratios. His goal is to improve those numbers	For political reasons, he needs to keep working with the systems of 3 different vendors	8	Include him in training sessions	Supply Chain Team Leader	☺
2	Ms. Terese Spencer	Finance	9	Financial Manager - Project member and main advisor of the CFO	She doesn't like some people in marketing	She thinks the project can give to much power to Marketing	Very outgoing and talkative. She speaks her mind	Financial planning and reporting - needs real time reports.	The layout of some reports must remain the same	5	Include her in the Marketing workshops and focus on common problems	Change Management Manager	☺
3	Mr. Larry Calisto	Supplier - Logistic	5	Small supplier of railcars. May be used in future phases of the project	No specific issue, but people in the company like him as a partner	He is afraid of restructuring.	He travels a lot. It is difficult to catch him on the phone. Secretary: Stacy	Maintain the company as a client	None	9	Align expectations	Supply Chain Team Leader/ Change Management Manager	☺
4	Mr. Sebastian Reggy	Retailer	7	Small retailer. The company may survive without him, but he may influence other retailers	He is one of the leaders of the association of the main retailers	He thinks the project is not taking into consideration the opinion of the retailers	He doesn't like consultants. He is very protective and result oriented	Improve the relationship between the company and the association of retailers	None	4	Sell the importance of the project and opportunities for improvements	Supply Chain Team Leader/ Project Manager	☺
5	Ms. Susan Ashton	CFO	10	Sponsor of the project.	She wants to achieve better interaction between the Finance and Marketing departments	She thinks the project will improve some specific business processes	People oriented, smart, and flexible. Always concerned about the suggestions of other departments	Measure the improvements after implementing the project in terms of EBITDA impact.	Every department must agree with the changes by signing off an agreement term.	8	Keep track of EBITDA.	Project Manager	☺

Figure 10: Example of Stakeholder Perception Map

The key issues column is used to describe points that deserve special attention while dealing with the stakeholder. The Perceptions column shows how the stakeholder perceives the project.

In the Perceptions column, the Project Manager tries to map what the stakeholder sees as the strengths, weaknesses, opportunities, and threats of the project. Based on this information, he may adjust his sales pitch to make the stakeholder accept the project.

A column with observations is also indicated to register the personal observations of the Project Manager regarding the behavior of the stakeholder. These observations may help the Project Manager to understand the actions of each stakeholder and create possible courses of action to overcome any problems.

Columns with Objectives and Constraints should be compared to the project goals and restrictions in order to create win-win situations.

The Overall Readiness for Change is a subjective measure of how willing the stakeholder is to accept any changes the project can bring. This can warn the Project Manager of possible problems, especially while considering the Relative Importance of each stakeholder.

Finally, in the last three columns, we have the action plan, those responsible in the project for following each stakeholder, and the status. The status is usually a visual sign indicating how pleased the stakeholder is with the current level of development of the project.

7.3 - Traditional Quality Tools

In 1947, William Edwards Deming arrived in Japan, taking with him a new approach to quality. He taught the Japanese many policies, procedures, and tools to use to improve the quality of their products and processes. That was the start of a new era in the business world: the Era of Quality.

After Deming, we saw many other gurus being recognized for their theories. People like Juran, Crosby, Ishikawa, and Feigenbaum made great contributions toward the development of quality in the world.

Some of the tools the "Quality Gurus" developed are used in many companies in order to identify, prioritize, describe, and analyze problems. Their quality tools allow workers everywhere to find the basic causes of problems and to develop an effective action plan.

There are many useful quality tools a Project Manager can use, but here I will present only my two favorite: Cause-and-Effect Diagram and Pareto Analysis. However, I strongly suggest that Project Managers read more about quality tools. They are usually simple and very effective.

Brassard [3] and Breyfogle [5] are good references for those willing to learn more about these tools.

Cause-and-Effect Diagram

Also called the Fishbone or Ishikawa Diagram, the Cause-and-Effect Diagram is designed to represent the relationship between an effect and all the possible causes that may contribute to this effect.

The analysis is presented in a graphic layout with the effect we want to investigate on the right side of the diagram and lines coming out of this effect in a fishbone shape. The fishbone splits into different categories where causes of the problem may be found.

The most traditional categories are manpower, machines, methods, materials, and environment. The categories are defined according to the kind of problem we analyze. In managerial areas, some suggested categories are policies, procedures, people, and layout.

After describing the effect stating what, when, and where the problem is happening, the Project Manager should define the possible categories related to the problem and brainstorm in each category to find possible causes.

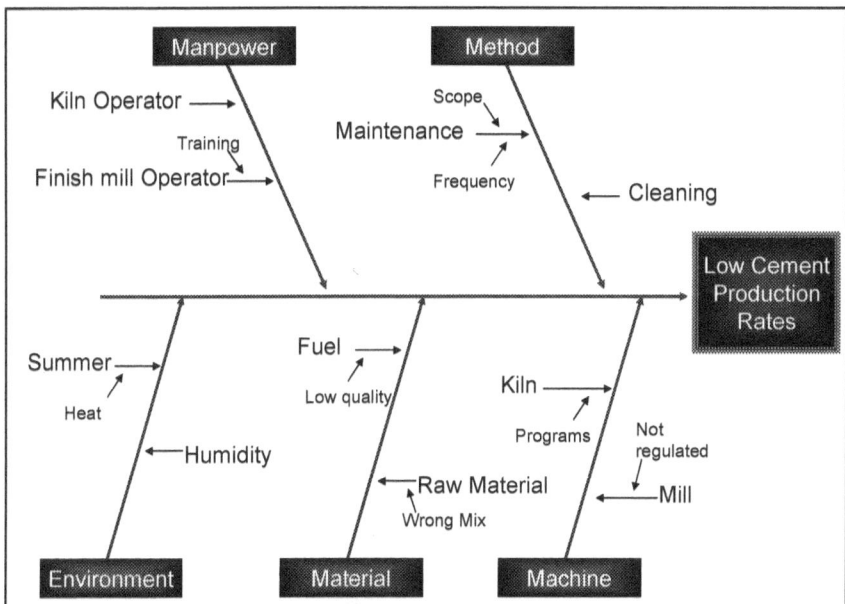

Figure 11: Example of Cause-and-Effect Diagram

Pareto Analysis

Pareto Analysis is a special form of chart consisting of vertical bars representing the number of times a specific event has happened. It allows us to compare the occurrence of different events (problems) in order to set priorities and focus on specific solutions.

Furthermore, the Pareto Analysis allows us to verify the 80–20 principle, which says that 80% of the problems are caused by 20% of the items. In other words, we should focus on a small number of important items.

The Pareto Analysis can use the ABC classification system (also known as the ABC curve). The problems are classified in three groups according to their occurrence. After ranking the problems, the first 80% of the occurrences are classified as the A group. This is the group that demands the maximum priority of the manager. The next 15% are classified as the B group. This is a group that requires certain attention. Finally, the remaining 5% are classified as the C group. This group shouldn't take too much of the manager's time.

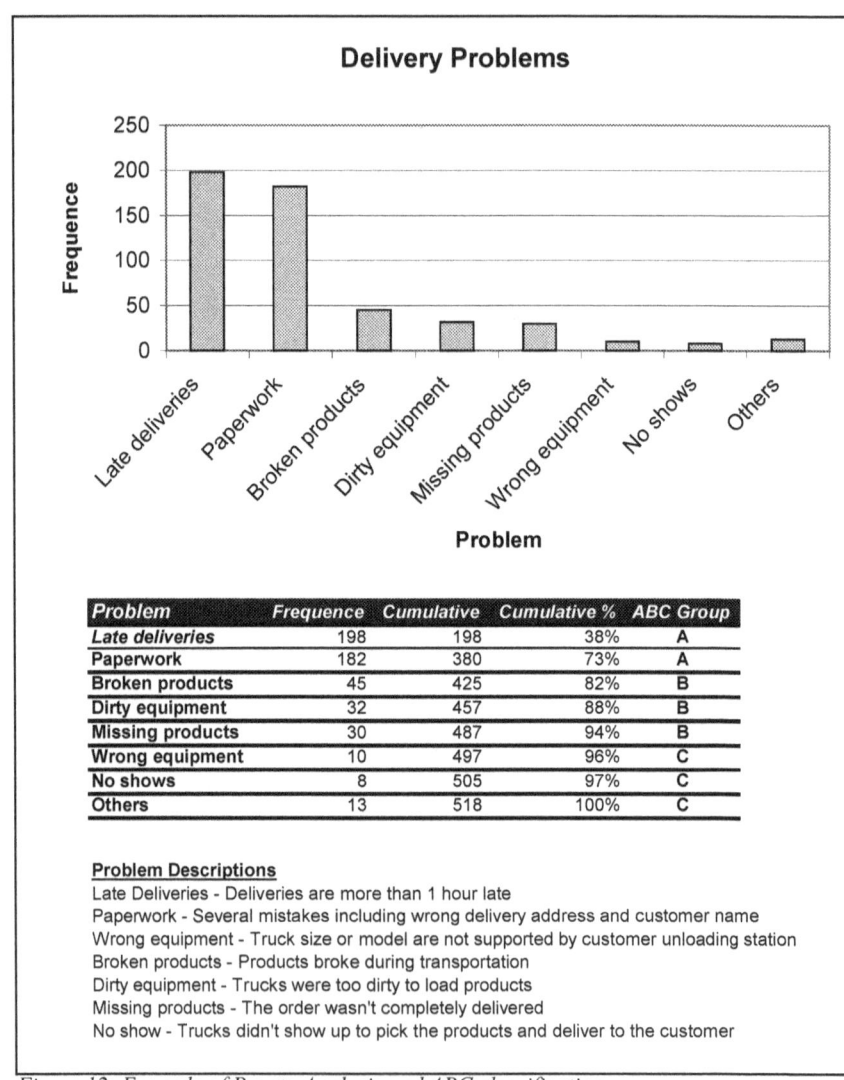

Problem	Frequence	Cumulative	Cumulative %	ABC Group
Late deliveries	198	198	38%	A
Paperwork	182	380	73%	A
Broken products	45	425	82%	B
Dirty equipment	32	457	88%	B
Missing products	30	487	94%	B
Wrong equipment	10	497	96%	C
No shows	8	505	97%	C
Others	13	518	100%	C

Problem Descriptions
Late Deliveries - Deliveries are more than 1 hour late
Paperwork - Several mistakes including wrong delivery address and customer name
Wrong equipment - Truck size or model are not supported by customer unloading station
Broken products - Products broke during transportation
Dirty equipment - Trucks were too dirty to load products
Missing products - The order wasn't completely delivered
No show - Trucks didn't show up to pick the products and deliver to the customer

Figure 12: Example of Pareto Analysis and ABC classification

Figure 12 shows an example of a Pareto Analysis and ABC classification for problems related to deliveries to customers. A Project Manager looking for a way to improve the quality of the deliveries would focus on the problems of Group A. The correction of these two problems would affect 73% of the occurrences.

Although this is a great tool, some people make a common mistake while analyzing the results of a Pareto Diagram. Sometimes, the frequency and type of problem don't reflect the impact they have. A problem with a low frequency can be more severe than a problem with a high frequency. For example, ten drunk drivers should deserve more attention than 200 late deliveries.

7.4 - Risk Assessment Chart

Risk can be translated as the chance of not achieving the desired result. For some non-critical activities, the risk may be more acceptable than for others. The Project Manager has to evaluate the main activities of the project and work toward the minimization of the risks. In addition, he should establish a contingency plan in case the threat of not achieving the expected result becomes a reality.

The more activities the Project Manager chooses to analyze, the safer the project will be. It is suggested that the Project Manager should analyze at least the activities in the critical path of the project (those that can impact the total length of the project) and those considered critical by the stakeholders. Characteristics of the project such as budget, retention of resources, and others may also be part of the points to be analyzed.

After selecting the activities to be analyzed, the next step in creating a Risk Assessment Chart is to identify the mode of failure. An activity may fail for not delivering the results on time or with the required quality, cost, or any other characteristic necessary to ensuring the success of the subsequent activities.

RISK ASSESSMENT CHART

#	Activity	Risk Description	Owner	Magnitude of Damage	Mitigation Plan	Contingency Plan	Risk Probability (1-9)	Risk Impact (1-9)	Risk Exposure
1	Raw Material Selection	The selected material may be expensive and the selected supplier may be abroad. If the supplier is abroad we may be exposed to currency rate flutuation.	Purchases Team Leader	The cost of the raw material may increase the cost of the product to unacceptable levels.	(1) Keep track of the costs. (2) Study a financial hedge to protect against currency rate flutuations.	(1) Change to a domestic raw material. (2) Study trade-offs between performance vs cost.	4	7	28
2	Technical Design of the Prototypes	They may not be ready on time (reason: marketing surveys used as input of the designers are usually late). In addition, none of the designs may please the customers.	Designers Team Leader	The whole project may run late	(1) Investigate and eliminate the reasons for delays in the marketing survey. (2) Add lead users to work with the designers to ensure the product will be satisfactory.	(1) Negotiate an extension in the project deadline and create additional designs	3	9	27
3	Production of Prototypes	We may not have the appropriate equipment to produce the prototypes in spite of our great variety of tools.	Manufacturing Team Leader	Impossibility of produce the prototypes.	(1) Follow the work of the designers and be sure to let them know of any restriction. Small adjustments in the design may solucionate this problem	(1) Lease/Acquire the necessary machines. Use emergency funds for that.	2	3	6
4	Marketing Survey to establish new product specifications	Marketing surveys are ususally late because of lack of available people with necessary knowledge in the company.	Marketing Team Leader	Possible delays and problems with the quality of the analyses.	(1) Hire and train new marketing analysts. (2) Use a third party to run the analyses - e.g. marketing agency	(1) If marketing is running late with their analyses, they should inform all the affected areas, so they can try to minimize the impact of any delay. (2) The Steering Committee should be communicated and a time extension in the project may be negotiated.	8	4	32
5	Retention Plan	Traditionally, many project members abandon the project in critical phases.	Project Manager	Delays in critical phases of the project. Lost of knowledge.	(1) Work harder on motivational tools. (2) Offer project conclusion bonus. (3) Prepare a succession plan for the team leaders. (4) Keep track of project documentation.	(1) Hire temps and additional personnel. (2) Use on-the-job training	8	8	64

Figure 13: Example of Risk Assessment Chart

The Project Manager may indicate the person responsible for keeping track of the risk of each activity. This person should be aware of the impacts the failure of the activity may have on the project. Besides, he may support the Project Manager on the creation and implementation of mitigation and contingency plans.

The Project Manager may attribute grades to each risk according to its probability of occurrence. He may use sophisticated statistical methods to calculate that probability or just make an educated guess using a 1 to 9 scale. Using the same idea, he may estimate a grade for the impact each risk may have on the project. With these two numbers (Risk Probability and Risk Impact), the Project Manager may create a Risk Matrix.

In the Risk Matrix, the Project Manager will plot the Risk Exposure of each process (Risk Exposure = Risk Probability x Risk Impact). That will allow the Project Manager to conduct a graphical analysis of the risks in order to focus on the activities with higher exposure. This is a prioritization tool.

Figure 14 brings an example of a Risk Matrix. As we can see, all the activities are plotted in the graph, which is divided into three different regions. The region in the top right corner indicates activities with high impact and probability of failure. Therefore, the Project Manager should concentrate his attention on these activities. The region in the middle indicates the activities that deserve some attention because they still represent some potential risk. The region in the lower left corner groups the activities with low impact and a low probability of failure. Thus, they shouldn't be the focus of the Project Manager.

The Project Manager should constantly evaluate the risks of each activity during the course of the project. Any change should be reflected in the Risk Assessment Chart and Matrix.

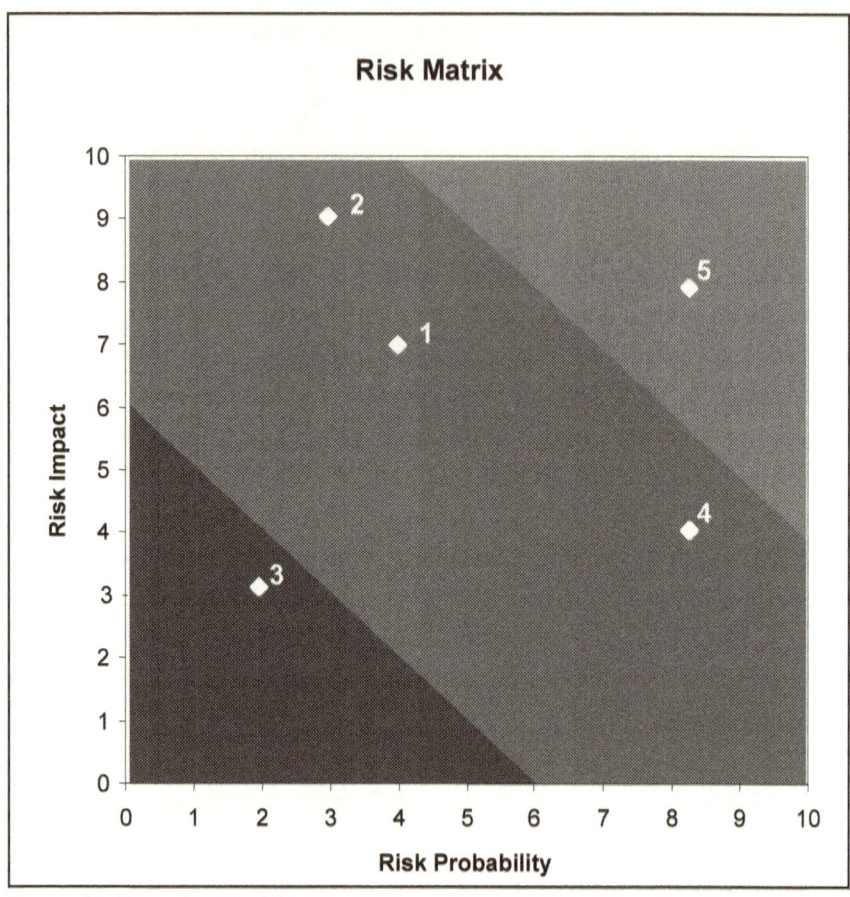

Figure 14: Example of Risk Matrix

7.5 - Six-Sigma Project Charter

As we showed in the second part of the book ("Concepts of Project Management"), the Project Charter is usually a thick document describing the goals, scope, schedule, and other important pieces of the project. However, the Project Manager should also have a way to present the main information of the project in a glance.

A "Six-Sigma Project Charter" is a tool used in some companies to summarize the main points of the Project Charter. It follows some concepts presented in the Six-Sigma philosophy.

Six-Sigma is a methodology used to eliminate defects in any process. Six-Sigma projects are usually executed by Six-Sigma Green Belts and Black Belts and may be overseen by Six-Sigma Master Black Belts. These are certified professionals who received extensive training in quality tools and Six-Sigma methodology to execute all kinds of projects.

Figure 15 shows an example of a Six-Sigma Project Charter. There are many different templates suggested in Six-Sigma books and websites. All of them bring similar information. We can observe the title of the project, the business case describing the reasons for creating the project, the goals, scope, team, project leader, milestones, and sponsor.

Note that the milestones are presented under the DMAIC approach. DMAIC is an acronym used in the Six-Sigma Philosophy that stands for Define, Measure, Analyze, Improve, and Control.

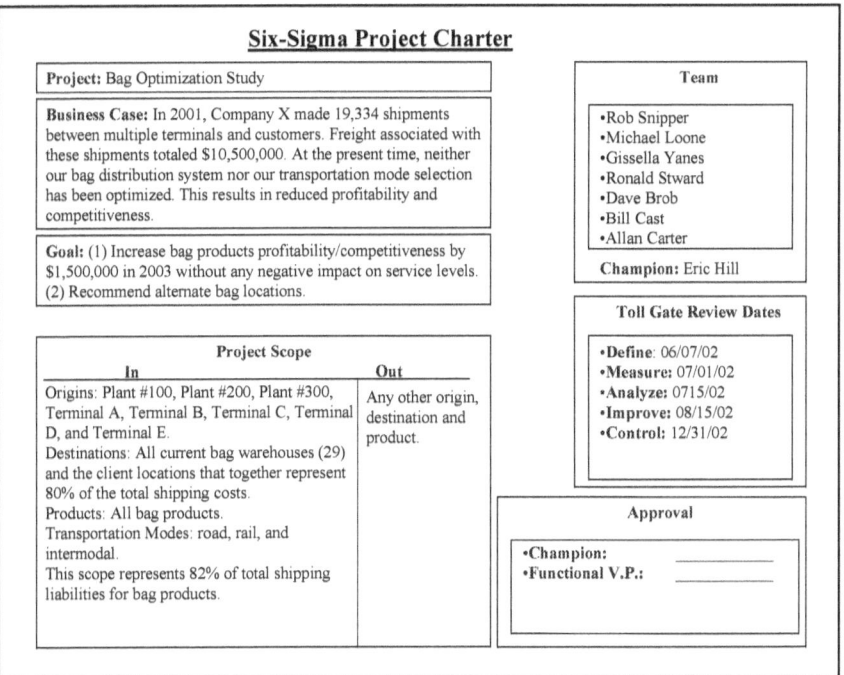

Figure 15: Example of Six-Sigma Project Charter

In the Define stage, we try to formulate the problem. In the Measure stage, we collect all the relevant data needed in order to understand the current state of the indicators that will be used to evaluate the success of the project. In the Analyze stage, we create the solutions for the problem. The Improve stage is where the solution is actually implemented. Finally, in the Control stage, we review the indicators initially measured to determine the success of the project.

In fact, these stages are more complex than these simple explanations. Project managers are strongly encouraged to consult additional resources in order to understand more about the Six-Sigma philosophy and tools.

Brefyfogle [5] and Pyzdek [23] are two great references for those willing to learn more about Six-Sigma.

8 – Intermediate Tools

When we talked about basic tools, we showed some different ways to group and present relevant information in a project. Other tools are not so straightforward. They actually require specific knowledge to be applied. In other words, we have to follow certain steps in order to transform the data before grouping and presenting the final results.

Some tools require a simple calculation, but they follow strict rules. These are the tools we are calling intermediate. In this chapter, we will present some of the main financial indicators used to decide on the implementation of a project and to measure its success. Furthermore, we will show the main aspects of a Gantt Chart and other network models. Finally, we will introduce the concept of the Quality Function Deployment (QFD), a tool used to transform customer preferences into technical requirements.

8.1 – Financial Indicators

There are many ways to decide on the implementation of a project. Generally, the decision is based on a series of components, such as feasibility and alignment with the corporate strategy. However, we may affirm that in 99.9% of the projects, a financial indicator is part of the criteria used to decide whether the project should be implemented or not. Consequently, every Project Manager has to be aware of the most common financial indicators.

The most common financial indicators are:

✓ NPV (Net present value)
✓ Payback
✓ IRR (Internal Rate of Return)

While making a decision, we should consider all of these indicators. A good NPV doesn't mean that the project should be implemented. For the same project, we may have a very unfavorable Payback.

Also, keep in mind that most financial indicators may be affected by taxes, depreciation, amortization, and other economical factors. A Project Manager should understand the nature of the project and which factors may impact the calculation of these indicators.

Brealey [4] does a good job describing these and other indicators like EVA (Economic Value Added).

NPV (Net Present Value)

The Net Present Value is a common method used to evaluate many projects. After estimating the future income and expenses of the project, we bring all these entries to present value by discounting the cost of capital (an interest rate to adjust for time and risk).

From the present value, we subtract the initial investment in order to find the Net Present Value. The NPV represents the value added by a project along its life. Therefore, a higher NPV indicates a better project.

For example, let's assume a simple project where we are buying a new machine. The new machine will allow our company to save money in the next five years, but it will also require additional maintenance. Figure 15 shows a table with the relevant values for this project.

As we can see, to calculate the present value, we discounted the cost of capital (6%) from each entry using the formula:

$$\text{Present Value} = \frac{\text{FutureValue}}{(\text{cost of capital} + 1)^{\text{Years}}}$$

The cost of capital used is the same interest rate used in investments available in the market with similar risk.

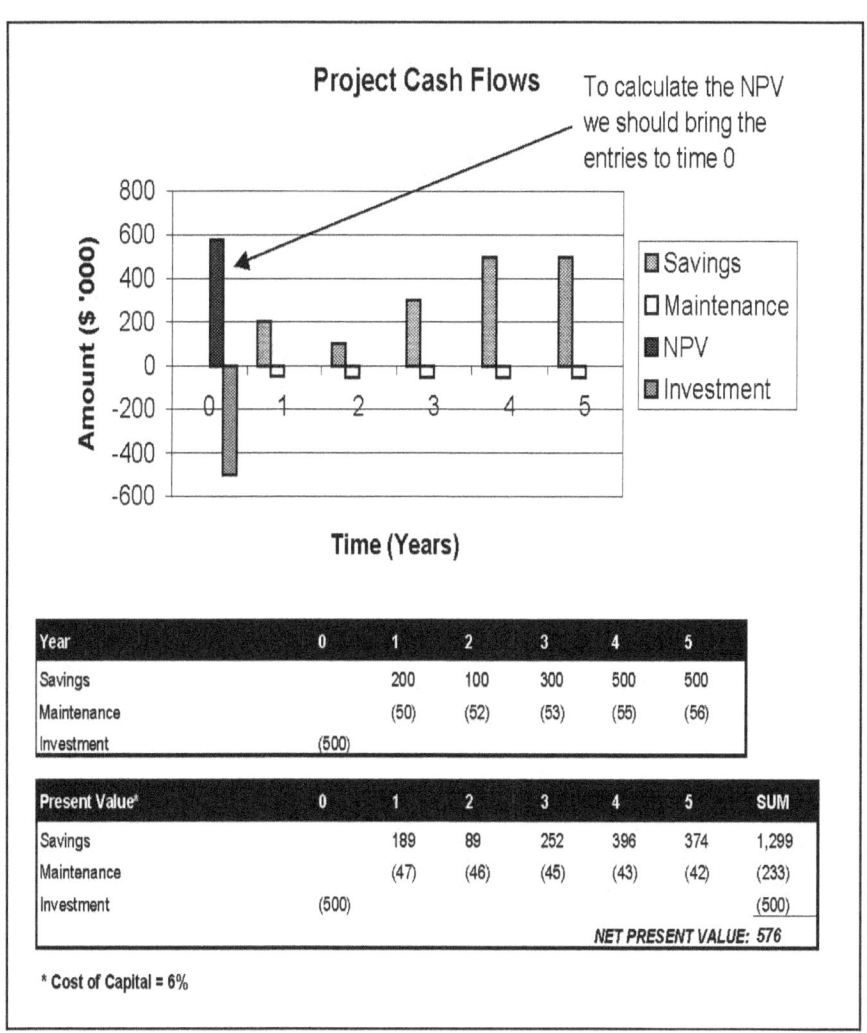

Figure 16: Example of Net Present Value calculation

PAYBACK

Would you invest $1 in a project with a Net Present Value of $100? It looks like a nice project, but what if the project took 100 years to generate a favorable cash flow? Now it probably doesn't look that attractive anymore.

Payback is another measurement used to estimate how long a project will take until the break-even point — the point where the accumulated income is higher than the accumulated investments and expenses.

The first step taken in order to calculate the Payback is to find the cash flows of each period of the project's life. The cash flow is the sum of all revenue (or savings) and expenses (or losses). Next, we have to bring the cash flow at present value, as described in the NPV methodology. We call this the Discounted Cash Flow.

Finally, we just have to add the cash flow from each year in order to find the Cumulative Discounted Cash Flow. The Payback is the length in years, months, or other time unit until the Cumulative Discounted Cash Flow becomes positive. Therefore, a small Payback indicates that we will see the benefits of the project at an earlier time.

Figure 17 uses the same example presented in the NPV explanation to calculate the Payback.

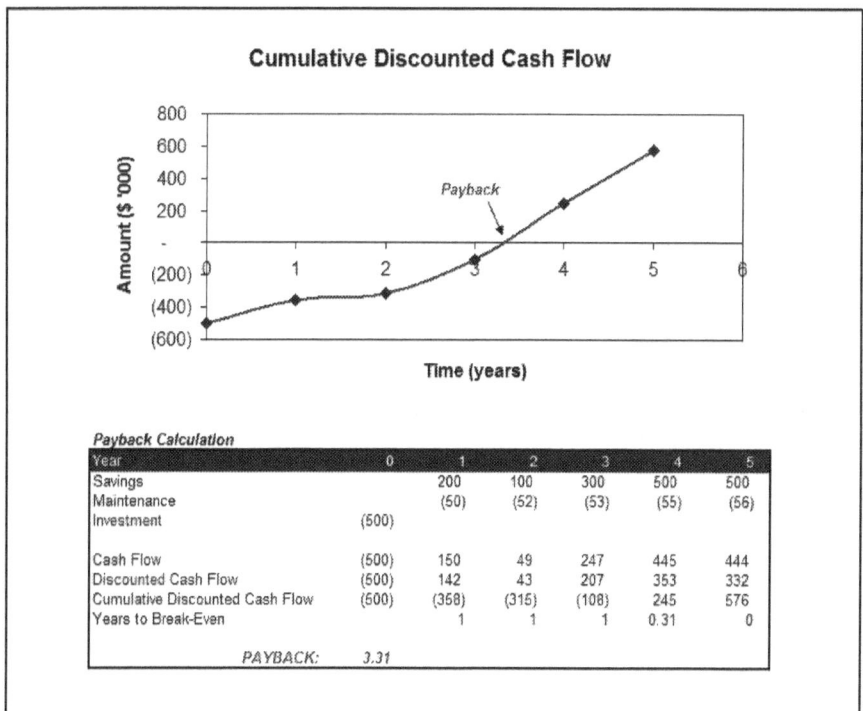

Figure 17: Example of Payback calculation

IRR (Internal Rate of Return)

The goal of the internal rate of return is similar to the Net Present Value. Both try to determine if the monetary return of the project is satisfactory. However, the NPV is expressed in monetary units, while the IRR is expressed as a percentage.

The IRR is the break-even rate of return. If the interest rate (cost of capital) of the project is smaller than the IRR, the NPV will be positive, indicating an acceptable project.

As we can see, the IRR has some advantages over the NPV. For example, it can be calculated without having to estimate the cost of capital.

Therefore, it is a good tool to use to compare different projects and investments.

Figure 18 uses the same example presented in the Net Present Value explanation to show the Internal Rate of Return. Note how the cumulative discounted cash flow ends at zero when we bring the entries to present value using the IRR as a discount rate.

IRR Calculation

Year	0	1	2	3	4	5
Savings		200	100	300	500	500
Maintenance		(50)	(52)	(53)	(55)	(56)
Investment	(500)					
Cash Flow	(500)	150	49	247	445	444
Discounted Cash Flow at IRR	(500)	113	28	106	144	109
Cumulative Discounted Cash Flow	(500)	(387)	(359)	(253)	(109)	0

IRR: 32.51%

Figure 18: Example of IRR calculation

8.2 - Gantt Chart

The Gantt Chart is a great tool to use to create a schedule and to track the progress of the activities. It shows a table with the activities displayed on the left in an indented structure and a graphical display using bars on the right, parallel to a horizontal timeline.

The first step taken in order to create a Gantt Chart is to identify the Work Breakdown Structure (WBS). The WBS is the hierarchic decomposition or breakdown of a project into successive levels, where each level is a finer breakdown of the preceding one. It is usually displayed in the form of a tree diagram or an outlined style and can be used not only for scheduling but also for budgeting and to create a network diagram.

Therefore, this project should be split into subprojects or milestones. A milestone represents the completion of correlated activities or events. Thus, we should understand all the deliverables of each phase of the project and mark them as a milestone.

The next step is to include in our project all the major activities necessary in order to achieve each milestone. Then, we can identify all the tasks associated with each of the major activities. For this, we use a top down approach. At each step, we try to increase the level of detail of the activities correlated to our project.

For example, in a Marketing Research Project where we want to send a survey to a selected audience and analyze their answers, we may have the following milestones: Project Kick-off Meeting, Audience Definition, Submission of Questionnaire, Answers Submission Deadline, Recommendations Due Date, and Executive Presentation.

After the Project Kick-off Meeting, the major activities needed in order to reach the Audience Definition could be Problem Investigation, Analysis of Competitors, and Data Compilation & Conclusions. Next, we would break these activities again into smaller tasks. We may use as many levels as necessary in order to ensure a good description of the project.

The next step is to define the relationship between activities. Some tasks depend on the conclusion of others in order to start. Some others need to start at the same time. The software used to create Gantt Charts can assign a number of relationships between tasks.

After identifying the relationship between the tasks, we may define the duration of each activity. Figure 19 shows an example of a Gantt Chart created with Microsoft Project®.

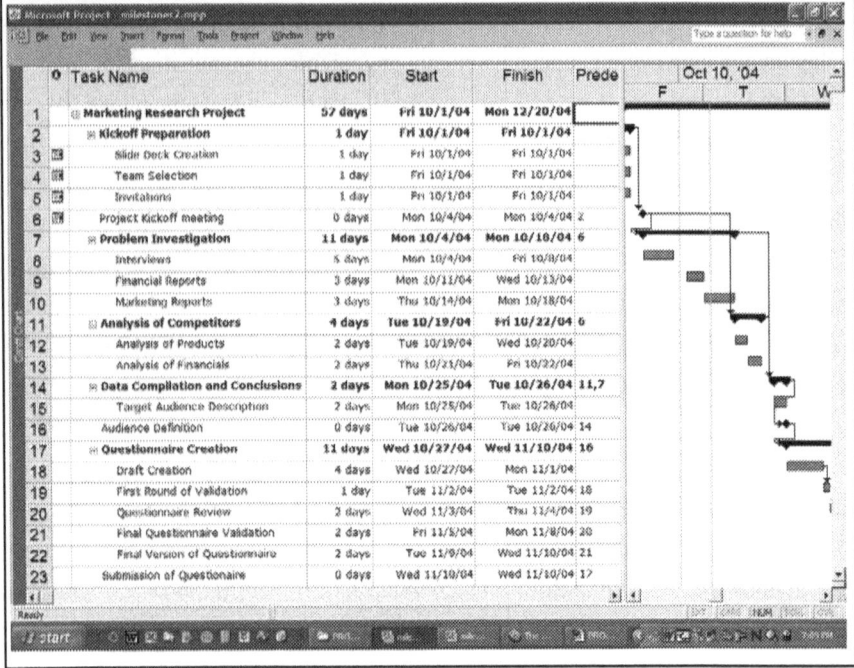

Figure 19: Example of Gantt Chart

With a push of a button, most project development software will also generate a Network Diagram. This kind of diagram shows the relationship between the tasks in a more graphical style. Some special kinds of network diagrams include the Performance Evaluation Review Technique (PERT) and CPM (Critical Path Method).

Both models, PERT and CPM, are very similar. The difference between them is in the time needed for each task. CPM simply takes the expected time, while PERT uses a weighted average between the best case, expected case, and worst case estimates to calculate the duration of each task.

The CPM model also highlights the Critical Path, which is the sequence of activities that should be prioritized since any delay in these activities would cause the delay of the entire project. Figure 20 shows the Network Diagram for our project.

After creating the Work Breakdown Structure, setting the duration of the tasks, and defining the relationships, we should name the person or group responsible for each task and plan the necessary resources.

Most of the software used for project management also has a great variety of standard reports to control schedule, budget, resources, and so on. Microsoft Project®, for example, has a table where we can add the information about each resource, including the cost. Based on the rate and usage, the software calculates the total cost of our project.

Figure 21 shows an example of a Resources Table and its effect on the Gantt Chart. In the figure, we can observe the updated information with the remaining cost of the project and each activity.

Some project management software also allows for "Resources Leveling" functionality. Although some activities may run in parallel, sometimes we need the same resource to run them. For example, independent activities may require the same financial analyst. Since they don't have a precedence order, the project may indicate that the financial analyst might need overtime in order to finish them. The "Resources Leveling" functionality moves activities in time, using the time between the activities in order to minimize the overtimes.

Figure 22 illustrates the concept behind Resources Leveling. Note that the system tries to postpone or pull forward the activities where the Financial Analyst 1 is allocated in order to reduce overtime.

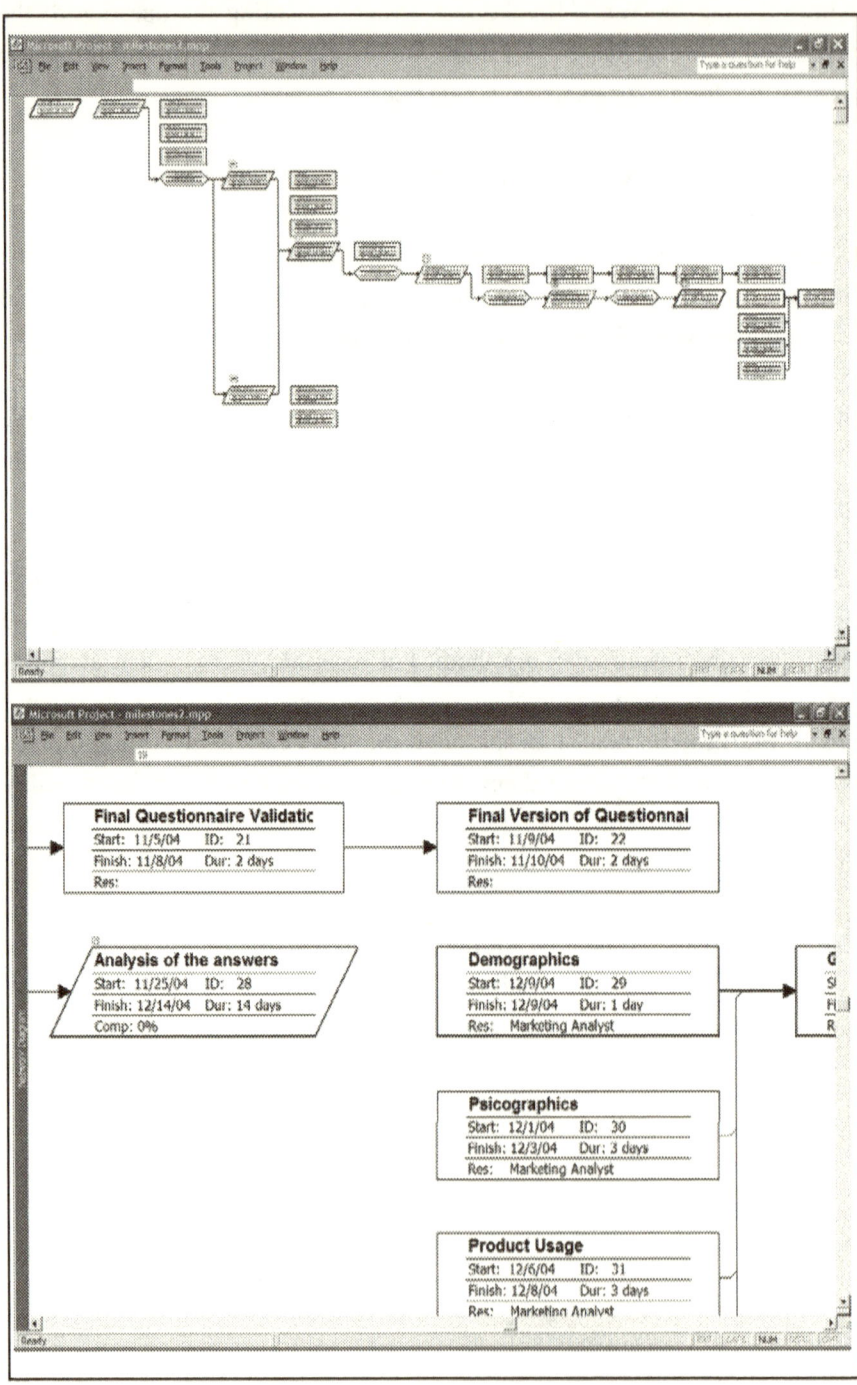

Figure 20: Example of Network Diagram – Overview and Detail

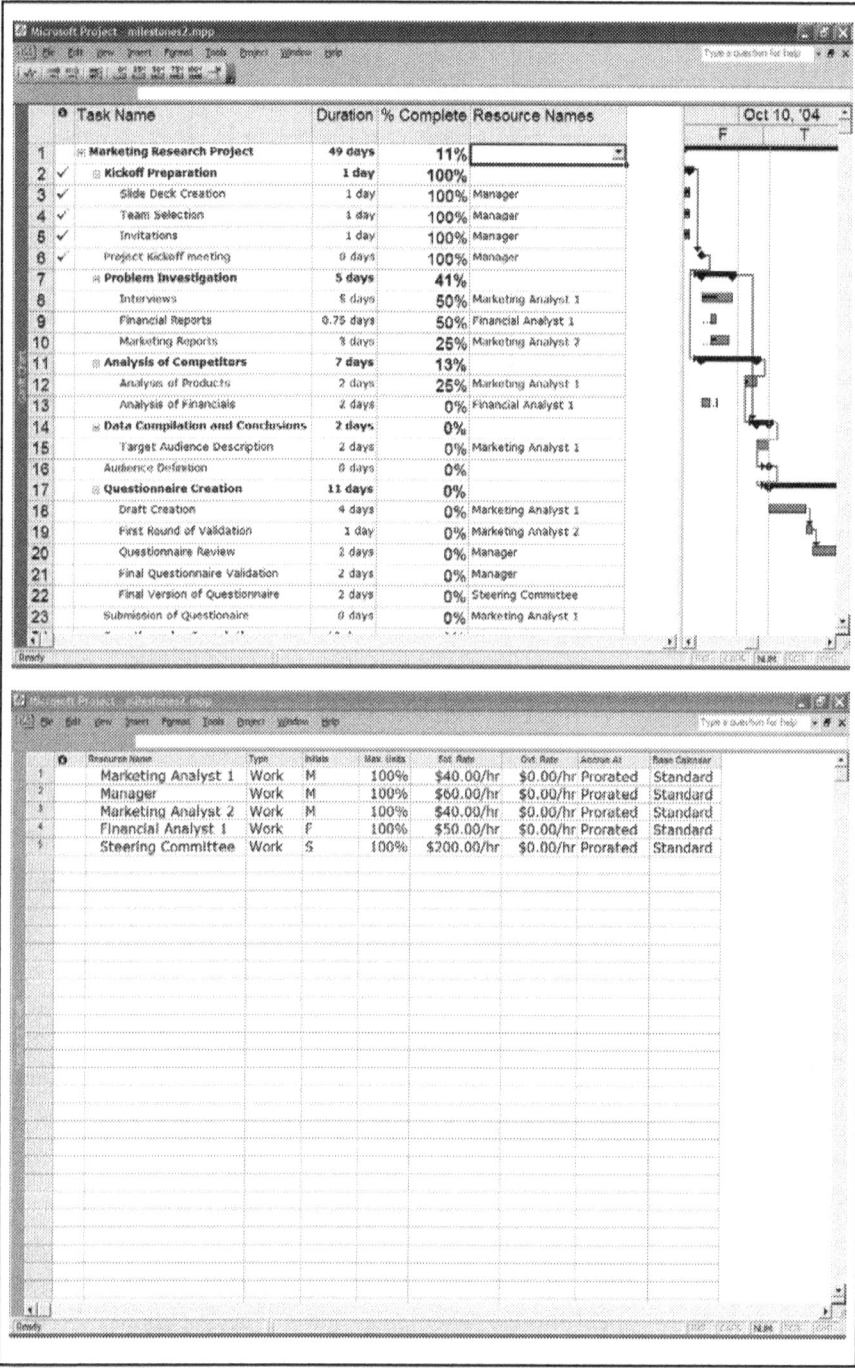

Figure 21: Example of Resource Allocation using a Gantt Chart

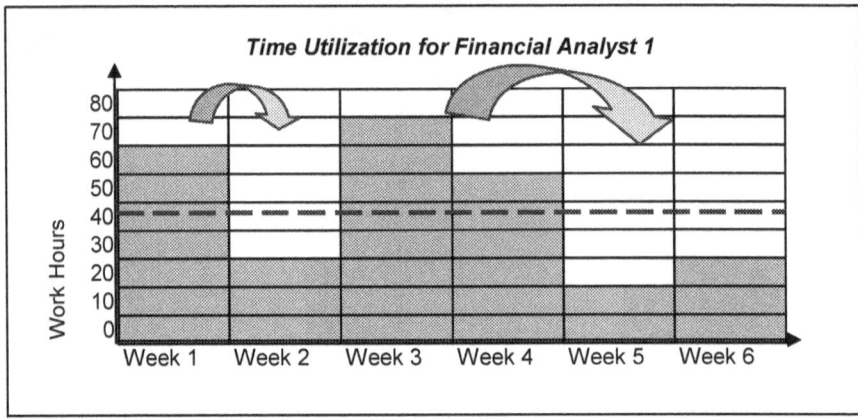

Figure 22: Resource Leveling Concept

Kerzner [18] is a great author for those looking for more information about scheduling and network models.

8.3 - Quality Function Deployment (QFD)

As we said in many parts of this book, communication is usually a big concern for the Project Manager. In fact, it is a huge issue in any corporation. If it is not easy to communicate within the company, imagine how hard it will be to communicate the point of view of a customer to the designing, engineering, and manufacturing departments.

The Quality Function Deployment (QFD) is a tool developed in the '60s to help improve communications between the customers and the production team. The QFD is applied during the early phases of projects in order to capture the preferences of the customer and incorporate them into the final product.

The QFD works with four matrices, where the customer preferences are deployed into Engineering Requirements, Parts Specifications, Process Operations, and Production Specifications, respectively.

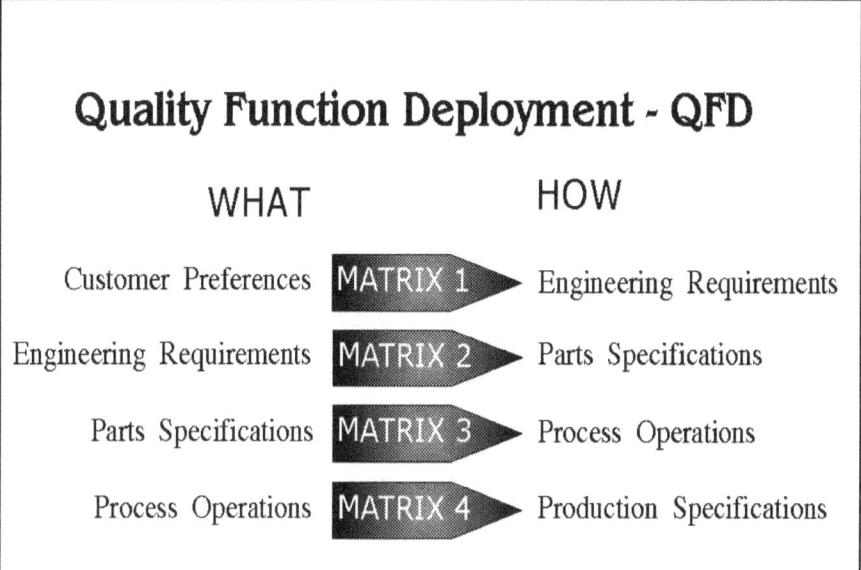

Figure 23: QFD Matrices Utilization

The first matrix is also known as the "House of Quality." Many times, companies work only with the first matrix. This matrix transforms customer preferences into engineering requirements. Figure 24 shows the layout of the House of Quality. However, note that sometimes only part of the boxes presented are used in an analysis.

The first step taken in order to develop the House of Quality is to establish customer preferences. This is usually done through surveys, interviews, observation, and other marketing techniques. These factors are usually called the "WHATs" representing "what" the customers want.

During this phase, the customers may also attribute different weights to each characteristic they seek in the product. These weights are defined according to the relative importance each characteristic has to the customer. In addition, the customers can describe the competitive positioning of each requirement related to the product or process been analyzed. This information feeds the customer ratings at the right box of the matrix.

Next, the Project Manager may conduct a brainstorm session with a multidisciplinary team formed of engineers, designers, and others to find the "HOWs." These are the engineering characteristics that could be changed in order to affect customer preferences.

In the "roof" of the House of Quality, we have a table with the tradeoffs among the different engineering requirements. In other words, this table shows how one engineering change may affect other characteristics. For example, the size of a battery may affect the energy it can supply.

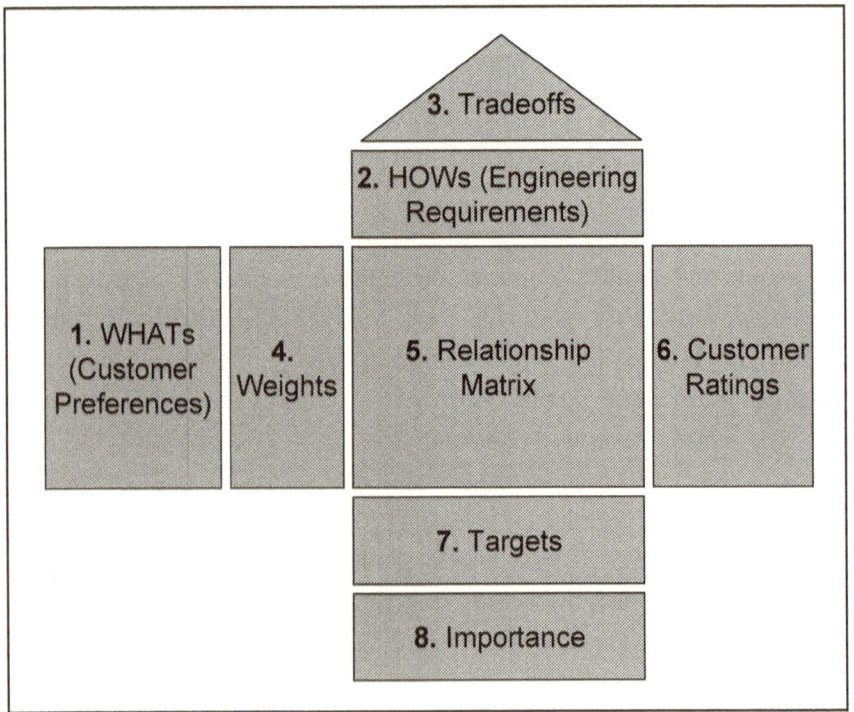

Figure 24: Layout of the House of Quality (QFD)

At the center of the "house," we have the relationship matrix. This indicates how each engineering characteristic affects each customer requirement. This can be done by attributing grades or positive and negative values.

At the bottom of the matrix, we have the targets for each engineering characteristic and the importance calculated using the weights and values in the relationship matrix.

This process continues to a second, third, and fourth matrix as the "HOWs" of one become the "WHATs" of the next. Figures 25, 26, 27, and 28 bring an example of the QFD matrices.

Although QFDs are usually applied in product development projects, a Project Manager may use the same concepts to transform the requirement of the clients in any project into technical specifications and constraints. Consequently, this tool can be adapted and used not only for products but also for processes.

Cohen [9] and Day [11] are good sources for those who want to learn more about QFD.

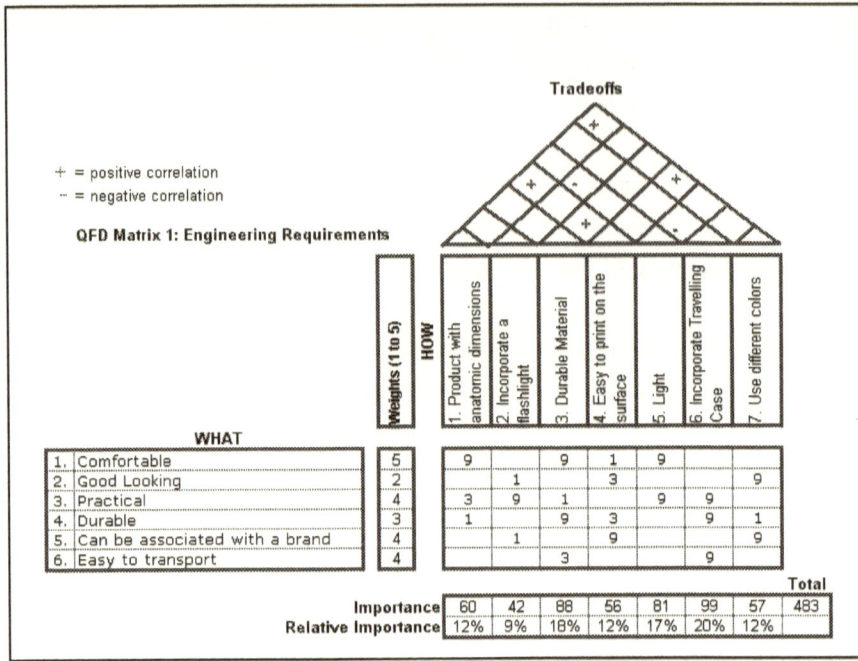

Figure 25: Example of the first matrix of a QFD

QFD Matrix 1: Engineering Requirements

+ = positive correlation
-- = negative correlation

WHAT	Weights (1 to 5)	1. Product with anatomic dimensions	2. Incorporate a flashlight	3. Durable Material	4. Easy to print on the surface	5. Light	6. Incorporate Travelling Case	7. Use different colors
1. Comfortable	5	9		9	1	9		
2. Good Looking	2		1		3			9
3. Practical	4	3	9	1		9	9	
4. Durable	3	1		9	3		9	1
5. Can be associated with a brand	4		1		9			9
6. Easy to transport	4			3			9	
Importance		60	42	88	56	81	99	57	483
Relative Importance		12%	9%	18%	12%	17%	20%	12%	

QFD Matrix 2: Parts Specifications

WHAT	Body		Flashlight		Composition	
	1. Right size of the body of the product	2. Smooth curves simulating the position of the fingers	3. Small flashlight	4. Good potency of flashlight	5. High density plastic	6. Good material to print on
1 Product with anatomic dimensions	9	9			1	
2 Incorporate a flashlight	1		9	9		
3 Durable Material		3			9	3
4 Easy to print on the surface	3				9	9
5 Light	3		3		3	
6 Incorporate Travelling Case	9		3			
7 Use different colors					9	9

Figure 26: Example of the second matrix of a QFD

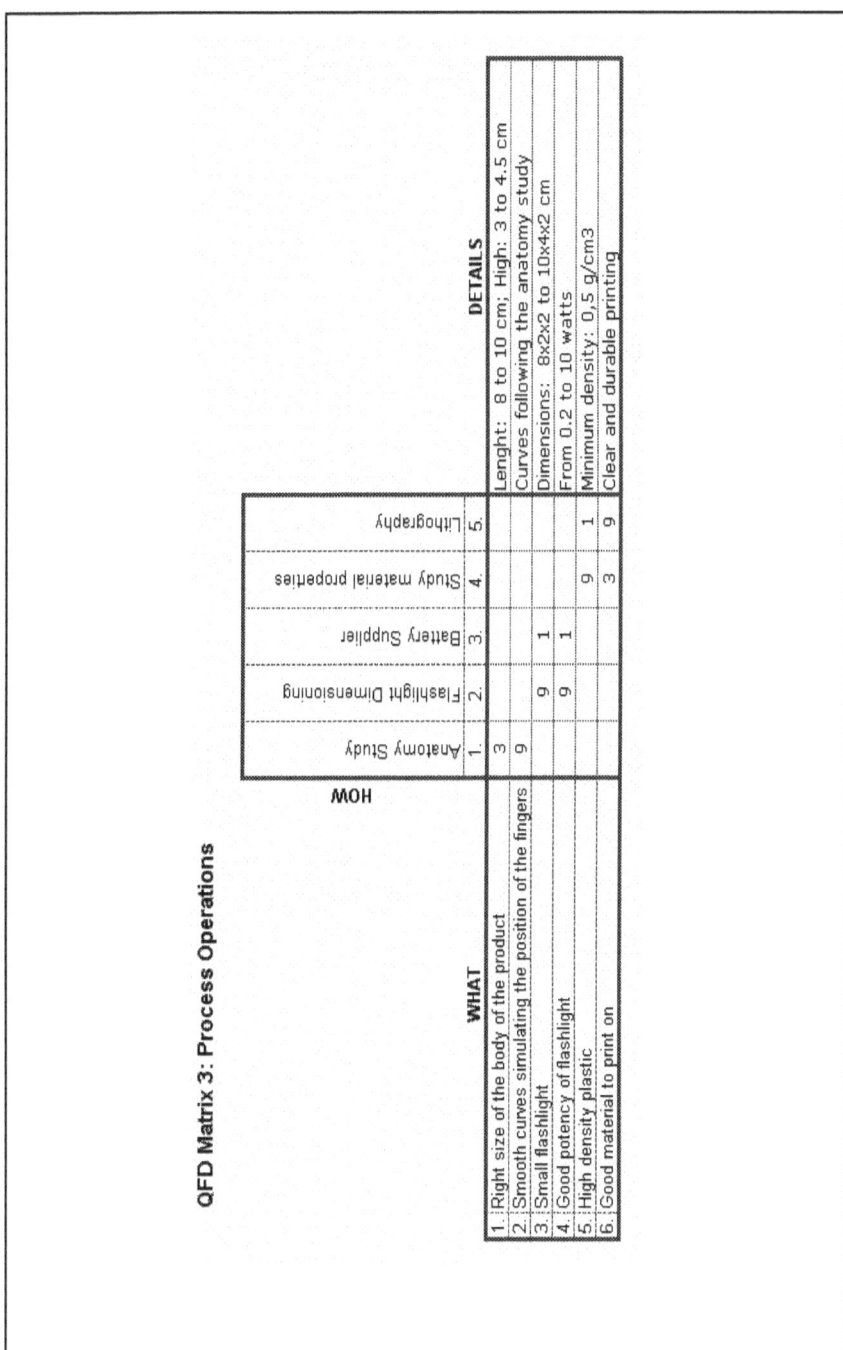

Figure 27: Example of the third matrix of a QFD

QFD Matrix 4: Product Specifications

1 Description	2 Flowchart	3 Deliverables in each task	Quality Control of the Product			Quality Control of the Process		
			4 Characteristics	5 Method	6 Frequency	7 Parameters	8 Method	9 Frequency
Anatomy Study	● Research ● Project of the product	Measures for hand anatomy Apply the study in the project						
Flashlight Dimensioning	● Analysis of the available room for the flashlight ● Definition of the size of the flashlight as per previous activity	Maximum size of flashlight Definition of the flashlight size						
Battery Supplier	● Research suppliers ● Acquisition ■ Inspection ● Transportation ▶ Storage of the material	List with qualified vendors Purchase of batteries Verify if specifications were met Material available at the plant Material in inventory						
Study material properties	● Study of main materials ● Material selection	List with the different properties of each material Definition of the best material						
Lithography	● Research printing methods ● Vendor Selection ● Order ■ Inspection ● Transportation ▶ Storage	Definition of the best method to print Select vendor for printing services Order the desired printings Verify if specifications were met Material ready at the plant Material in inventory						

Figure 28: Example of the fourth matrix of a QFD

9 – Advanced Tools

So far, we have seen some straightforward tools that group and present data and some other tools that require some skill and a little calculation. These kinds of tools are enough to help the Project Manager in 99.9% of the cases faced.

Nevertheless, there are many other powerful tools that can support the decisions and analyses of the Project Manager in several different situations. These tools can give more flexibility and credibility to the analyses and results. However, they may require strong mathematical skills and a deep knowledge of the concepts.

In this chapter, we present three great tools: Real Options Analysis, Optimization Models, and Regression Models for Surveys.

Real Options Analysis is an advanced technique used to support managerial decisions based on the outcomes and probabilities of different future scenarios. For example, the Project Manager may have to decide between continuing or abandoning a project according to partial results and the probabilities of certain events that may happen in the future. The Real Options Valuation may support this kind of decision, among many others.

Optimization Models can be applied in many different cases. Almost every company uses some sort of logistics optimization system to define the most economical way to move their products. A Project Manager can use optimization models in many situations. For example, he can use it to select from a project portfolio the ones he should work on and prioritize.

Regression Models are commonly used as a forecast tool to predict the behavior of a series. However, a Project Manager can use the statistical concepts behind the regressions to analyze the result of surveys.

In the business and academic world, we may find many different tools to help a Project Manager. Some of them are easy to apply and some are very difficult. However, anyone can learn how to use a tool, but that is not enough. The successful Project Manager should know not only how but also when to apply each tool. Besides, when facing a new challenge, he may have to use his creativity and other skills to adapt these tools and tackle new problems. It may take some time for a Project Manager to develop this kind of skill. The best advice I can give is to keep practicing, keep trying new things, and keep studying. Knowledge is an endless quest.

9.1 - Real Options

Real Options Analysis, also know as Real Options Valuation, is a very advanced technique used to support the decision making process. A Real Options Analysis may be conducted when we have a certain degree of flexibility in future phases of a project.

For example, to build a new distribution center for a company, we have many phases. The initial step is the acquisition of the land. Next, we may have the design of the building, the creation of a blueprint, and the construction. At the end of each phase, we may decide to abandon the project by selling the land with any construction we may have started. The decision may be based on the changes in the market affecting future revenues.

For instance, we may decide to abandon our project if a competitor starts shipping his products to the region where we are building our distribution center by taking advantage of a change in the freight prices. On the other hand, the freight prices may increase, making the product of the competitors more expensive, so our project becomes more attractive.

In a traditional Net Present Value analysis, we wouldn't be able to analyze all the different scenarios in order to make a decision. So, we usually analyze only the most likely scenarios. We may opt to analyze more than one scenario using NPV, but we would end up with one NPV to each scenario. We can also try to combine the NPV from different scenarios using a weighted average based on the probability of occurrence for each scenario. However, only the Real Options Analysis considers the flexibility we have in the future (e.g., to abandon the project) to answer whether we should accept this project or not.

In fact, we can use Real Options Analysis for many different kinds of decisions. Besides the abandonment option, we may want to analyze a deferral option (e.g., we may want to postpone the decision of whether to continue with a project), a scope contraction (e.g., we may want to reduce the size of our project), a scope expansion, and so on.

There are a few different methods used to analyze Real Options. However, the theories behind the analyses are very complex. They are based on financial market theories (stocks and portfolios). Two of the most known methods are the Replicating Portfolio and the Risk-Neutral Approach.

My goal is not to explain these theories. This is an extensive subject and many other authors do an excellent job of explaining the details behind Real Options Analysis. My objective here is to show an example of how a Real Options Analysis can be used in a project. This may open a new world for a Project Manager dealing with similar problems. There are many good references I could suggest for those who want to become a specialist in Real Options. However, I strongly suggest starting with a basic investments book before moving to a Real Options book.

Bodie, Kane, and Marcus [2] do an excellent job of explaining the concepts of the financial market, while Copeland and Antikarov [10] focus on practical application and theories or Real Options. These books are strongly recommended for those who want to understand more about this method.

Let's analyze a practical example. Imagine that a Project Manager was asked to analyze and conduct a one-year project. The total investment is $200K, and the present value of the revenue it will generate is $195K.

However, the market where the final product of the project will be commercialized is very unstable, and revenue could easily change. Throughout the year, the project management will have two opportunities to abandon the project and sell all the assets for $180K.

A simple NPV analysis would show us $5K in losses, since the total investment is $200K for a projected revenue of $195K. Therefore, our first reaction is to reject the project. However, in this analysis, we wouldn't be considering the flexibility of selling the assets for $180K.

The first step for a Real Options Analysis is to create a decision tree, with the present value of the revenue. This tree has three levels. The first represents the present value of the project (revenue). The second level shows the value of the project considering two different scenarios (favorable and unfavorable market variations) at the first opportunity for selling the assets in the future. The third level shows all the possible outcomes of the project at the second chance of discontinuing the project. Figure 29 shows the decision tree.

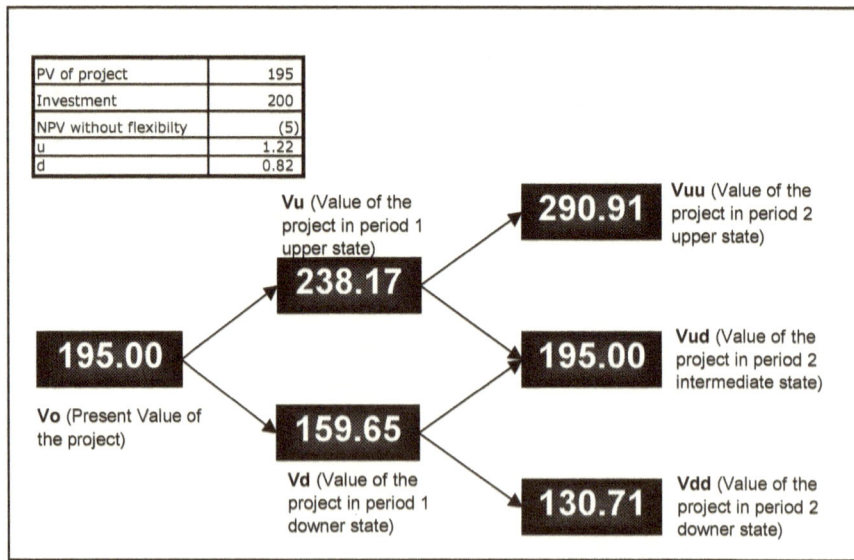

Figure 29: Example of Decision Tree with 20% volatility

As we can see, at the end of the project, our expected revenue in the worst case is $131K, but we have the option of selling the assets for $180K. Therefore, we should exercise our option and abandon the project. This new expected revenue at the third level will impact the expected revenue at the second and third levels. Figure 30 shows the new decision tree with the value of the option exercised at the end of the project.

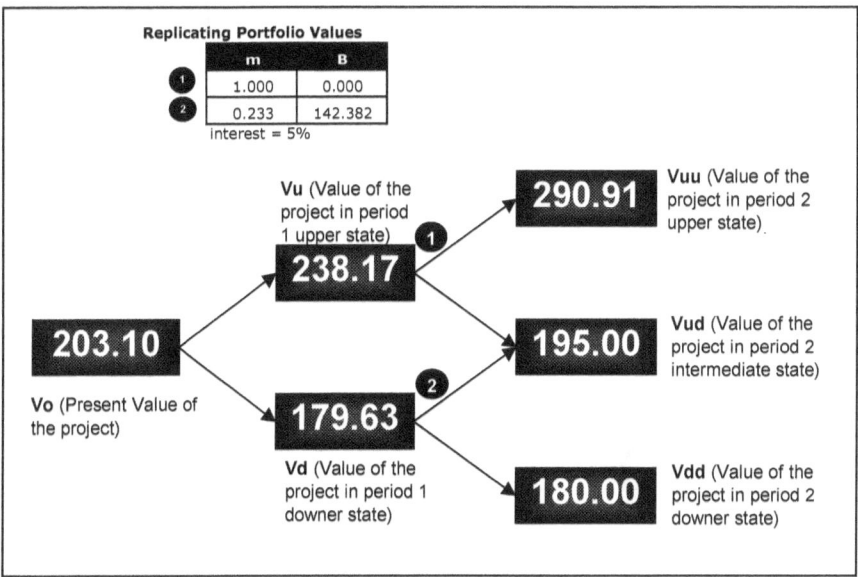

Figure 30: Decision Tree with option executed at the third level

Note that after we exercise our option at the third level of the tree, we still have revenue at the second level. This revenue is less than the $180K we may get by abandoning the project and selling the assets. Therefore, we should also abandon the project in the first opportunity we have, if the pessimistic scenario becomes true.

By abandoning the project and selling the assets at the second level of the tree, we will affect the first level, too. Figure 31 shows the final decision tree.

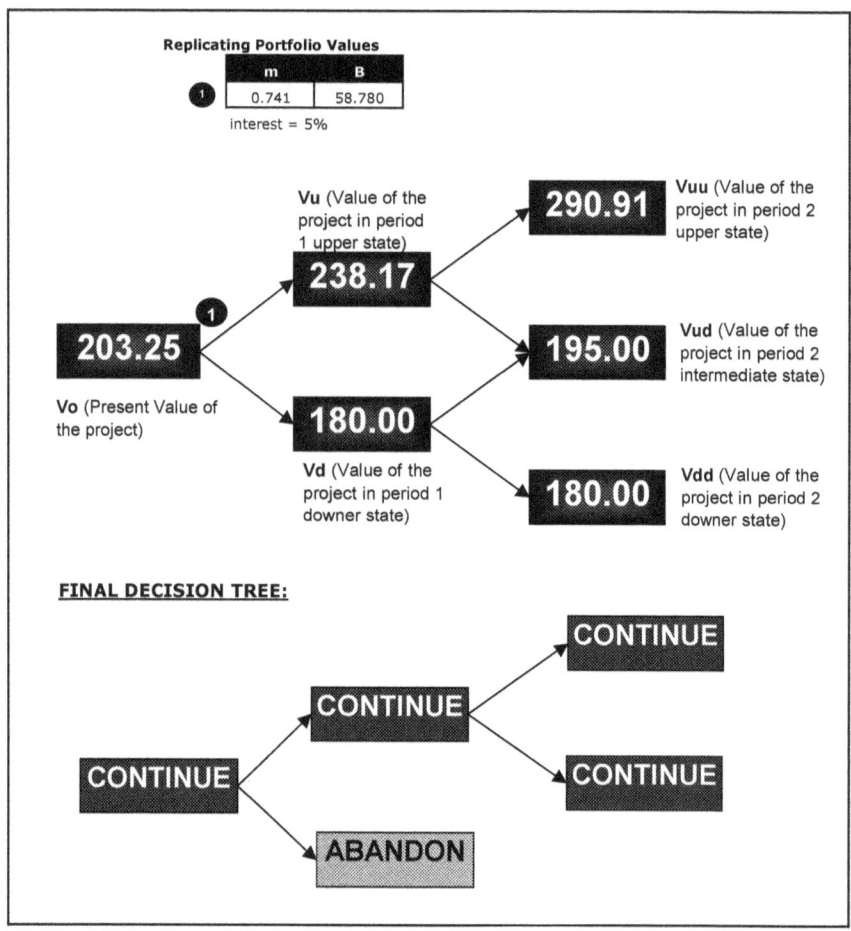

Figure 31: Final Decision Tree

As we can see, the project that started with a NPV showing a loss of $5K is now showing a favorable NPV of $3.25K after using the Real Options Analysis. This variation is due to the option of abandoning the project.

This was a very simple example, but it serves to illustrate how powerful the Real Options Analysis is. By analyzing possibilities of expansion, contraction, abandonment, and others, a Project Manager may accept projects that he would initially reject.

9.2 - Optimization Models

Nine years ago, I was taking my first optimization class in college. My professor was teaching us how to solve a basic optimization problem with a technique called "Simplex." Computers were not widely available, so we were calculating all the necessary steps for the simulations using small calculators. It used to take me more than 30 minutes to do what we can now do in just a few seconds with a computer.

Thanks to the development of technology, many advanced tools are available to anyone with a computer and some knowledge. Professionals everywhere look for the best way to accomplish their tasks. They want the most profitable way, the most economical, the fastest, and the one providing the least amount of risk. Optimization is a reality in today's business and personal environments.

One of the first optimization problems I tried to solve was called "The Boy Scout Problem." A boy scout was going to camp for a week, and he had to select what to take with him. However, he had limited space in his backpack. So, he measured each item and attributed a relative importance to each one. The boy used an optimization model to maximize the value of the items he was taking with him (maximized the importance) considering the capacity limitation.

The Boy Scout chose the resources he was going to need considering a specific restriction. Using the same reasoning, a Project Manager can choose resources for his project considering other constraints.

Every optimization problem is formed of two parts: goal, or optimization function, and constraints. The optimization function states the characteristics we want to maximize, minimize, or set to a specific value. Profits, availability of machines, number of accidents, and cost are examples of characteristics we may want to maximize or minimize.

Constraints are boundaries that restrict our solution. For example, we may want to maximize profits from a specific project, but we may have only a small amount of money to invest or a few man-hours available. Typical constraints are money, labor, time, and capacity.

Look to the table in Figure 32. It shows all proposed projects in a specific company with a three-year payback. The table also shows the necessary investment, man-hours, and Net Present Value. Imagine that you are a Project Manager, and you have to decide which projects to accept, assuming you can invest only $5 million and 9,000 hours of your project team. The high executives of the company asked you to maximize the Net Present Value. Which projects would you accept?

CONSTRAINTS				
Available Investment Money ($'000):		5,000		
Available Man Hours:		9,000		
Project	NPV ($'000)	Payback	Investment	Man Hour
P1	1,500	3	300	1,100
P2	1,800	3	350	1,200
P3	1,300	3	280	800
P4	1,900	3	380	1,300
P5	1,100	3	400	600
P6	850	3	300	500
P7	890	3	200	800
P8	980	3	300	350
P9	560	3	400	250
P10	1,900	3	800	1,000
P11	4,000	3	1,200	2,800
P12	4,300	3	1,500	2,500
P13	800	3	200	300
P14	500	3	300	200
P15	955	3	400	450
P16	1,220	3	300	600
P17	660	3	100	200
P18	800	3	250	250
P19	880	3	280	200
P20	190	3	50	100

Figure 32: Example of an optimization problem

This is not an easy exercise to solve on a piece of paper, but it becomes very simple using a program with optimization features. Remember that in this problem, we are not considering factors such as the possibility of overtime or the possibility of using a third party to run some of the projects. Furthermore, our decision is only based on Net Present Value. For example, we could try to construct a complex model considering also the reduction of the risk exposure.

The first step in solving this problem is to create variables representing the acceptance of each project or not. Using these variables, we can create our optimization function. Figure 33 shows the mathematical model used in this optimization. The result is displayed in Figure 34.

In this example, we have created a very simple optimization model to define the best projects a Project Manager should select for his portfolio. However, there are many other areas where this knowledge can be applied by a Project Manager, including logistics, supply chain, finances, and marketing. Only the creativity of the Project Manager can limit the usage of this tool.

Chong and Zak [8] can be helpful for those who want to take a first step into optimization models.

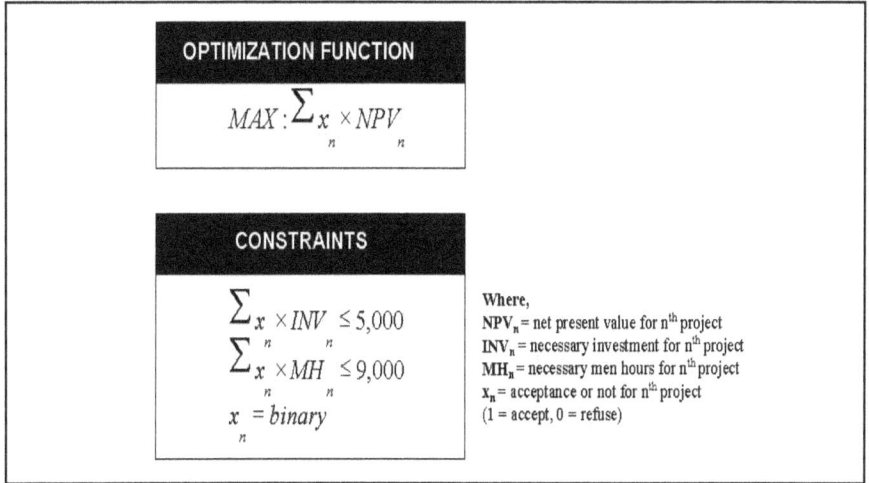

OPTIMIZATION FUNCTION

$$MAX: \sum_n x_n \times NPV_n$$

CONSTRAINTS

$$\sum_n x_n \times INV_n \leq 5,000$$
$$\sum_n x_n \times MH_n \leq 9,000$$
$$x_n = binary$$

Where,
NPV_n = net present value for n^{th} project
INV_n = necessary investment for n^{th} project
MH_n = necessary men hours for n^{th} project
x_n = acceptance or not for n^{th} project
(1 = accept, 0 = refuse)

Figure 33: Example of mathematical formulation of an optimization problem

OPTIMIZATION FUNCTION

MAX Total NPV:	$ 17,135

CONSTRAINTS

Available Investment Money ($'000):	5,000
Available Man Hours:	9,000
Total Investment ($'000):	4,990
Total Man Hours:	8,950

Project	NPV ($'000)	Payback	Investment	Man Hour	Accept Project?
P1	1,500	3	300	1,100	0
P2	1,800	3	350	1,200	1
P3	1,300	3	280	800	1
P4	1,900	3	380	1,300	1
P5	1,100	3	400	600	0
P6	850	3	300	500	1
P7	890	3	200	800	0
P8	980	3	300	350	1
P9	560	3	400	250	0
P10	1,900	3	800	1,000	0
P11	4,000	3	1,200	2,800	0
P12	4,300	3	1,500	2,500	1
P13	800	3	200	300	1
P14	500	3	300	200	1
P15	955	3	400	450	1
P16	1,220	3	300	600	1
P17	660	3	100	200	1
P18	800	3	250	250	1
P19	880	3	280	200	1
P20	190	3	50	100	1

Figure 34: Result of the optimization problem used as example

9.3 - Regression Models for Surveys

Statistics is taught in many courses in college, such as engineering, biology, and law. There is a reason why this subject is part of so many different careers. Statistics are a universal tool. You can apply them to many different situations.

Regressions are usually used as a forecast tool. For example, based on factors such as inflation rate, average income, new house starts, and others, it is possible to predict how many washing machines will be sold in a specific market.

Although this is the traditional use of regressions, a Project Manager should be able to adapt tools like this so that they may be used in other situations. One good example is the use of regressions in satisfaction surveys.

In many projects, the Project Manager will have to analyze the final result of a project or measure the satisfaction of the stakeholders along the way so that he can adjust the activities and deliver a better result. Consequently, satisfaction surveys are a reality in many projects.

In many companies, the typical satisfaction survey consists of a questionnaire where the interviewee classifies his satisfaction for different items in a numerical scale. For instance, the interviewee may classify the courtesy of the technical support staff on a scale from 1 (terrible) to 10 (excellent). The results of the surveys are usually presented as a simple average, showing the attributes which need to improve.

This approach has many problems. For example, we may not be capturing all the attributes or at least the most important — those impacting on the satisfaction of the interviewees. In addition, we may have no clue about the importance of each characteristic. Therefore, we may focus our efforts on improving a characteristic that is not important.

Let's review a small example of how statistics can be used to improve this analysis. Let's consider a Project Manager trying to measure the satisfaction level of the first part of a specific project. In order to do that, he decides to conduct a survey among the stakeholders. The results of this survey will give the Project Manager the information needed to develop the second part of the project.

Let's assume that the Project Manager starts with a hypothesis that the main dimensions affecting the satisfaction of the stakeholders are the speed of the project, the perceived quality of the final solution, how it was delivered, improvements brought by the project, and cost.

After that, the Project Manager creates questions to evaluate different characteristics related to the dimensions he proposed. Figure 35 shows an example of a basic questionnaire structure the Project Manager might use. Of course, the questionnaire should present detailed explanations of each item to ensure that each interviewee understands what is being evaluated and what each grade represents. In addition, the Project Manager has to decide on the best method of distributing the questionnaires (e.g., e-mail, web site, hard copy, interview) and collect the results.

To analyze the survey data, the Project Manager may count on different statistics software. The first step should be the execution of correlation matrices between the attributes or characteristics and their respective dimensions and between the dimensions and overall satisfaction.

The results of the matrices will show how each variable correlates to the other. For instance, we will know how much of the effort on "Courtesy" will actually affect the satisfaction associated with the "Delivery." A positive correlation means that the higher the courtesy index, the better the satisfaction with delivery will be. However, a correlation of 0.5 doesn't mean that every 1 point of improvement in courtesy will improve 0.5 points in "Delivery."

Another function of the Correlation Matrices is to analyze for Multicolinearity. This is a statistical aspect when the variables used to run a regression are highly correlated. As you can see, this is not a simple tool.

There are many basic introductory books to statistics. Hastie, Tibshirani, and Friedman [13] do a good job of introducing the main concepts to most of the statistical analyses. However, I recommend Hair, Bush, and Ortinau [12] for those who want to see the statistics concepts under a marketing approach.

OVERALL IMPRESSION

Please classify how satisfied you were with the following aspects of the project in a scale from 1 (Completely dissatisfied) to 5 (Completely Satisfied):

A – Overall Project Satisfaction	*1*	*2*	*3*	*4*	*5*
B – Implementation Speed	*1*	*2*	*3*	*4*	*5*
C – Overall Quality	*1*	*2*	*3*	*4*	*5*
D – Delivery Method	*1*	*2*	*3*	*4*	*5*
E – Improvements	*1*	*2*	*3*	*4*	*5*
F – Total Cost	*1*	*2*	*3*	*4*	*5*

SPEED

G - Implementation Time	*1*	*2*	*3*	*4*	*5*
H - Assisted Operation Time	*1*	*2*	*3*	*4*	*5*

QUALITY

I - Documentation Quality	*1*	*2*	*3*	*4*	*5*
J - Technical Solution	*1*	*2*	*3*	*4*	*5*
K - Project Team Knowledge	*1*	*2*	*3*	*4*	*5*

DELIVERY

L - Courtesy	*1*	*2*	*3*	*4*	*5*
M - Responsive to questions	*1*	*2*	*3*	*4*	*5*
N - Accuracy	*1*	*2*	*3*	*4*	*5*

IMPROVEMENT

O - People Improvement	*1*	*2*	*3*	*4*	*5*
P - Processes Improvement	*1*	*2*	*3*	*4*	*5*

COST

Q - Training Cost	*1*	*2*	*3*	*4*	*5*
R - System Maintenance Cost	*1*	*2*	*3*	*4*	*5*
S - Resources Cost (People)	*1*	*2*	*3*	*4*	*5*
T - Equipment Cost	*1*	*2*	*3*	*4*	*5*

Figure 35: Example of Questionnaire Structure

Figure 36 shows an example of a correlation matrix while Figure 37 shows the hierarchical display of the dimensions with the respective correlations.

Pearson Correlations

	Overall Satisfaction	Speed	Quality	Delivery	Improvement	Cost
Overall Satisfaction	1	0.589	0.834	0.724	0.875	0.862
Speed	0.589	1	0.497	0.611	0.512	0.415
Quality	0.834	0.497	1	0.733	0.792	0.749
Delivery	0.724	0.611	0.733	1	0.504	0.573
Improvement	0.875	0.512	0.792	0.504	1	0.889
Cost	0.862	0.415	0.749	0.573	0.889	1

Figure 36: Example of a Correlation Matrix

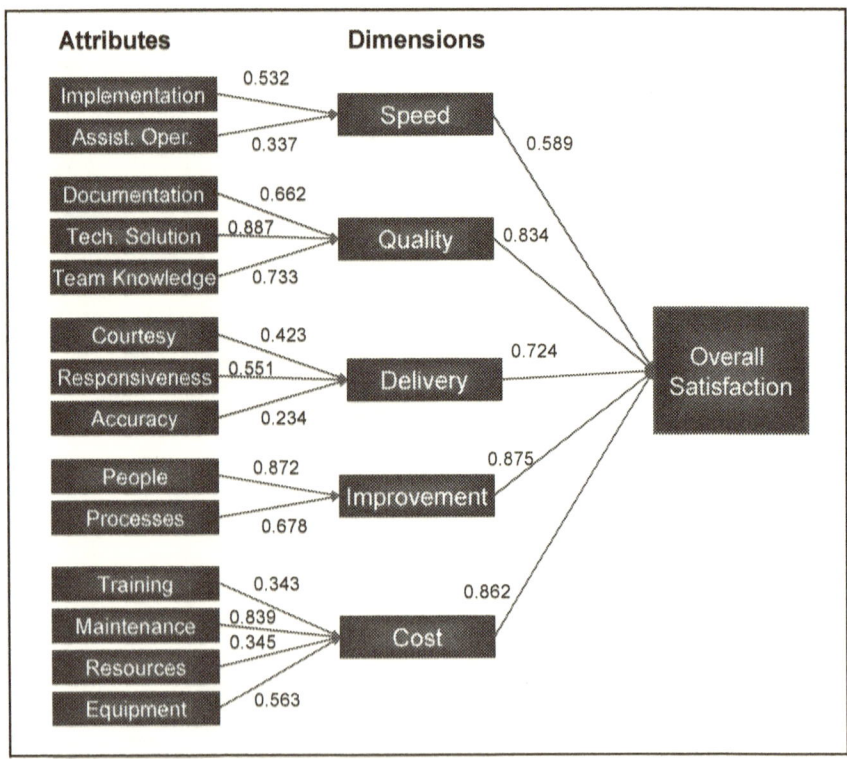

Figure 37: Example of hierarchical display of the dimensions with correlations

While researching the statistical tools that can be applied to this model, you may also want to check Factor Analysis. This analysis can validate the way we group our attributes into dimensions and suggest new ways to group them. Consequently, we may come up with new dimensions.

After analyzing the correlations, we may run a regression using as dependent variable the overall satisfaction and the dimensions as independent variables. It means the equation resulting from our regression would try to predict the overall satisfaction based on the dimensions we have defined.

We will also run regressions for the dimensions using the attributes as independent variables. An example of the result of a regression is presented in Figure 38.

Regression Statistics				
R Square		0.78142		
Standard Error		0.32343		
Observations		200		

	Coefficients	Standard Error	tStat	P-value
(Constant)	-0.32851	0.37032	-0.88709	0.00020
Speed	0.07265	0.14250	0.50984	0.00000
Quality	0.06080	0.18782	0.32372	0.00001
Delivery	0.28388	0.16568	1.71344	0.00032
Improvement	0.43320	0.20648	2.09807	0.02003
Cost	0.31809	0.19517	1.62981	0.01042

Figure 38: Example of regression results

As we can see in Figure 38, the result of the regression brings us the information needed in order to create the equation used to predict the behavior of the overall satisfaction. The same approach should be taken to calculate the regression in order to predict the behavior of the dimensions based on the attributes.

In addition, we have an R Square of 0.78. This means that our model was able to explain 78% of the behavior of the overall satisfaction. A low R Square would indicate that our dimensions were unable to explain the overall satisfaction. Therefore, we would have to improve our questionnaire and define new dimensions.

According to the data on Figure 38, the final equation for the Overall Satisfaction should look like this:

Overall Satisfaction = -0.32851 + 0.07265 x Speed + 0.06080 x Quality + 0.28388 x Delivery + 0.43320 x Improvement + 0.31809 x Cost

Note that the most important factor in our regression is Improvement, since for each one unit we improve in cost, the overall satisfaction improves 0.4332. Thus, this information may help the Project Manager to understand where he should focus his attention.

He may decide to create an importance/performance chart, as displayed in Figure 39. In one axis of the chart, we have the relative importance of each dimension (the weights found during the regression analysis). In the other axis, we have the simple average of each dimension representing the current performance. The Project Manager should focus his attention on moving the high importance dimensions with low performances (area 1) to the high performance area (area 2) and maintain those who are already in that area.

Based on the equations, the Project Manager can also analyze possible tradeoffs between the dimensions. If he knows how the dimensions relate to one other, he may even create an optimization model to define the best tradeoffs.

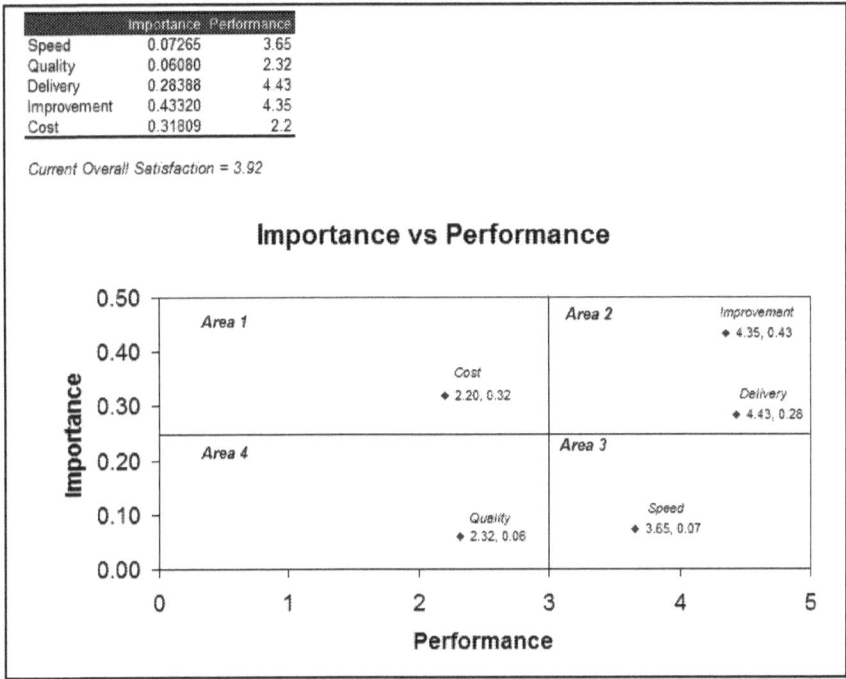

	Importance	Performance
Speed	0.07265	3.65
Quality	0.06080	2.32
Delivery	0.28388	4.43
Improvement	0.43320	4.35
Cost	0.31809	2.2

Current Overall Satisfaction = 3.92

Figure 39: Example of an Importance/Performance Chart

As we can see, there are many possible ways to analyze a satisfaction survey. Once again, the creativity of the Project Manager is the only limitation for a good analysis.

Bibliography:

[1] Baker, Sunny and Kim, and Campbell, G. Michael, 3rd Edition. *The Complete Idiot's Guide to Project Management.* New York. Alpha

[2] Bodie, Z, Kane, A., and Marcus, A. J., 5th Edition. *Investments.* McGraw-Hill

[3] Brassard, Michael, ed. 1985. *Qualidade - Ferramentas para uma Melhoria Contínua - The Memory Jogger[TM].* Rio de Janeiro, RJ. Qualitymark Editora Ltda.

[4] Brealey, Richard A., and Myers, Stewart C., 6th Edition. *Principles of Corporate Finance.* McGraw-Hill

[5] Breyfogle III, F. W., 2nd Edition. *Implementing Six Sigma: Smarter Solutions Using Statistical Methods.* Wiley

[6] Butler, Kirt C., 3rd Edition. *Multinational Finance.* South-Western College Publishing

[7] Champoux, Joseph E., ed. 2000. *Organizational Behavior: Essential Tenets for a new Millennium.* South-Western College Publishing

[8] Chong, E. K., Zak, S. H. 2nd Edition. *An Introduction to Optimization.* Wiley-Interscience

[9] Cohen, Lou, 1st Edition. *Quality Function Deployment.* Prentice Hall PTR

[10] Copeland, T., and Antikarov, V., ed. 2001. *Real Options.* New York, TEXERE LLC

[11] Day, Ronald G., ed. 1993. *Quality Function Deployment: Linking a Company With Its Customers.* ASQ Quality Press

[12] Hair Jr., J. F., Bush, R. P., and Ortinau, D. J., 2nd Edition. *Marketing Research.* McGraw-Hill

[13] Hastie, T., Tibshirani, R., Friedman, J. H., ed. 2001. *The Elements of Statistical Learning.* Springer-Verlag

[14] Hill, C. W. L., and Jones, G. R., 5th Edition. *Strategic Management Theory.* Houghton Mifflin Company

[15] Holland, W. E., Holland, D., 1st Edition. *Red Zone Management.* WinHope Press

[16] Hull, John C., 4th Edition. *Fundamentals of futures and options markets.* New Jersey. Prentice Hall

[17] Kaplan, R. S., Norton, D. P., ed. 1996. *The Balanced Scorecard: Translating Strategy into Action.* Harvard Business School Press

[18] Kerzner, Harold, 8th Edition. *Project Management: A Systems Approach to Planning, Scheduling, and Controlling.* Wiley

[19] Kleinbaum, D. G., Kupper, L. L., Muller, K. E., Nizam, A., 3rd Edition. *Applied Regression Analysis and Multivariable Methods.* Brooks Cole

[20] Lang, H. J., Merino, D. N., ed. 1993. *The Selection Process for Capital Projects (Wiley Series in Engineering and Technology Management).* Wiley-Interscience

[21] Lunn, T., Neff, S. A., 1st Edition. *Material Requirements Planning: Integrating Material Requirement Planning and Modern Business.* McGraw-Hill

[22] Niven, Paul R., 1st Edition. *Balanced Scorecard Step-by-Step: Maximizing Performance and Maintaining Results.* Wiley

[23] Pyzdek, Thomas, 2nd Edition. *The Six Sigma Handbook, Revised and Expanded: The Complete Guide for Greenbelts, Blackbelts, and Managers at All Levels.* McGraw-Hill

[24] Spunt, Trevor M., ed. 2003. *Guide to Customer Surveys: Sample Questionnaires and Detailed Guidelines for Creating Effective Surveys.* Customer Service Group

[25] Wainright, Gordon, 2nd Edition. *Teach Yourself Body Language.* McGraw-Hill

[26] Wallace, T. F., Kremzar, M. H., ed. 2001. *ERP: Making It Happen: The Implementer's Guide to Success with Enterprise Resource Planning.* Wiley

www.ingramcontent.com/pod-product-compliance
Lightning Source LLC
Chambersburg PA
CBHW021941170526
45157CB00003B/879